Press

Medals, Ribbons and Unit Awards of the U. S. Army Vietnam

Dedicated to all Vietnam veterans and their families who supported them when they so unselfishly served their country in the United States Army.

E Book Edition ISBN - 978-1-884452-87-1
Softcover Edition ISBN - 978-1-884452-88-8

Copyright 2024 by MOA Press

All rights reserved. No part of this publication may be reproduced, stored in retrieval systems or transmitted by any means, electronic, mechanical or by photocopying, recording or by any information storage and retrieval system without permission from the publishers, except for the inclusion of brief quotations in a review.

Press

Published by:

MOA Press (Medals of America Press)
114 Southchase Blvd. • Fountain Inn, SC 29644
www.moapress.com • www.usmedals.com

Medals, Ribbons and Unit Awards of the U. S. Army Vietnam

Table of Contents

Introduction 2
Types of Medals, Ribbons and Attachments 3
Army Military Ribbon Wear Guide 5
U.S. Army Pyramid of Honor 11
South Vietnamese Military Medals and Ribbons 38
Commemorative Medals and Ribbons 44
Claiming Military Medals and Ribbons 46
Veterans' Medals Displays 48

Introduction

Military medals, ribbons, and unit awards hold significant importance to the American soldiers who served during the Vietnam War as well as for their families and friends.

Decorations and campaign medals symbolize the veterans' and their fellow soldiers service and sacrifice when serving in the Vietnam War. Many veterans faced incredibly challenging and dangerous situations during their Vietnam tour of duty and these awards acknowledge their commitment to duty and the sacrifices they made.

For soldiers who demonstrated exceptional courage, bravery, and dedication, receiving medals and ribbons provides validation of their valor. These decorations serve as tangible reminders of their bravery in the face of adversity, offering a sense of pride and honor.

Military medals and ribbons are often awarded for specific achievements or accomplishments during service, such as acts of heroism, meritorious service, or participation in significant campaigns or operations. Each of these awards commemorate the individual and collective achievements of soldiers and units during the Vietnam War.

Military awards also contribute to a sense of belonging and identity among veterans. They signify membership in a select group of individuals who shared similar experiences and challenges during their military service in Vietnam. For many veterans, wearing their medals and ribbons is a source of pride and a way to connect with fellow Vietnam veterans.

For families of soldiers who made the ultimate sacrifice during the Vietnam War, receiving posthumous awards and decorations honors their loved one's memory and recognize their veteran's service and sacrifice. These medals serve as a lasting tribute to those who gave their lives in service to their country.

Military medals and ribbons serve as a legacy for veterans, preserving their stories and experiences for future generations. They ensure that the contributions and sacrifices of Vietnam War veterans are not forgotten and continue to be remembered and honored by subsequent generations.

The military medals, ribbons, and unit awards in this book are important symbols of valor, sacrifice, and service for Vietnam War veterans and their families. They represent not only individual achievements but also the collective courage and dedication of those who served during this tumultuous period in our history.

"The story of our Army during the Vietnam war through its awards for Valor, Merit and Service "

Types of Medals, Ribbons and Attachments

Decoration - *An award conferred on an individual for a specific act of gallantry or for meritorious service.*

Medal - *An individual award presented for performance of certain duties or to those who have participated in designated wars, campaigns, expeditions, etc., or who have fulfilled specified service requirements.*

There are two general categories of "medals" awarded by the United States to its military personnel, namely, decorations and service medals.

The terms *"decoration"* and *"medal"* are used almost interchangeably today *(as they are in this book)*, but there are recognizable distinctions between them. Decorations, are awarded for acts of gallantry and meritorious service and usually have distinctive *(and often unique)* shapes such as crosses or stars.

Medals are awarded for good conduct, participation in a particular campaign or expedition, or a noncombatant service and normally come in a round shape. Campaign or service medals are issued to individuals who participate in particular campaigns or periods of service for which a medal is authorized. The fact that some very prestigious awards have the word *"medal"* in their titles *(e.g.: Medal of Honor)*, can cause some confusion.

Attachments and Devices

Attachment - Any device such as a star, clasp, or other appurtenance worn on a suspension ribbon of a medal or on the ribbon bar (also called device).

Bronze and Silver Service / Campaign Stars
A bronze star is worn on suspension ribbons of large and miniature medals and ribbon bars to indicate a second or subsequent award or to indicate major engagements in which an individual participated. Silver Stars - A silver star is worn on suspension ribbons of large and miniature medals and ribbon bars in lieu of five bronze stars.

Letter "V"
A bronze letter "V" is worn on specific combat decorations if the award is approved for valor (heroism). Only one "V" is worn and oak leaf clusters are used to indicate additional awards.

Army Occupation Service Medal Clasp
The bronze Army of Occupation Medal clasp marked "GERMANY" and or "JAPAN" is worn on suspension ribbons of large and miniature Army of Occupation Medals to denote service in those areas.

Oak Leaf Cluster
A bronze Oak Leaf Cluster denotes a second or subsequent award of a personal decoration. A silver Oak Leaf Cluster is worn in lieu of five bronze Oak Leaf Clusters.

Hour Glass
A bronze hour glass device denotes ten years service on the Armed Forces Reserve Medal. Upon the completion of the ten year period, reservists are awarded the Armed Forces Reserve Medal with a bronze hourglass device. Silver and gold hourglass devices are awarded at the end of twenty and thirty years of reserve service, respectively.

Letter "M"
A bronze letter "M" on the Armed Forces Reserve Medal denotes reservists mobilized and called to active duty.

Airplane
The Berlin Airlift Device, a three-eighths inch gold C-54 airplane, is authorized to be worn on the ribbon bar and suspension ribbon of the Army Occupation Service Medal by Personnel who served 90 consecutive days in support of the Berlin Airlift (1948-1949).

Bronze Numerals
Denotes total number of awards of the Air Medal and other awards.

Bronze Arrowhead
Denotes participation in parachute, glider or amphibious landing or assault.

Good Conduct Medal Clasp
Number of loops and color denote number of awards of Good Conduct Medal. Bronze, 2nd - 5th; silver, 6th - 10th; gold, 11th - 15th.

Unit & Ribbon Only Awards

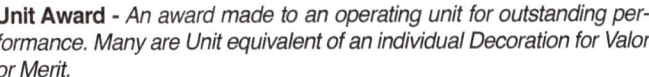

Unit Award - *An award made to an operating unit for outstanding performance. Many are Unit equivalent of an individual Decoration for Valor or Merit.*

Ribbon Only Award - *An award made to an individual for completion of certain training or specific assignment for which there is no medal. There were no ribbon only awards during Vietnam.*

Medals of America Press

★ Military Medal Variations

- Regulation Ribbon Bar
- Miniature Medals
- Enamel Lapel Pins
- Enamel Hat Pins (unofficial)
- Miniature Medals Anodized or Gold-Plated
- Miniature Ribbons (unofficial)
- **FULL SIZE MEDALS**
  - Bronze
  - Anodized or Gold-Plated
- Brass Plates — VIETNAM SERVICE

Decorations are announced in official military orders. The orders are filed in an individual's military record jacket and retired to a records holding area when the individual is discharged or retired. A decoration usually comes with a citation, certificate and boxed medal with ribbon and lapel pin.

Authorization for service medals are noted in an individual's official military records. They are generally issued in a small cardboard box. Ribbon-only awards and unit citations are sometimes issued but generally the individual has to purchase them. Foreign medals, such as the Republic of Vietnam Campaign Medal are generally required to be purchased by individual service members.

Announcement of the decoration is published in official orders.

Republic of Vietnam's Gallantry Cross Award Certificate and Orders.

4 Medals, Badges and Insignia U.S. Army Vietnam

U.S. Army
Military Ribbon & Medal Wear Guide
Order of Precedence and Attachments of U.S. Army Medals and Ribbons

Vietnam service with silver campaign star (5 campaigns) on Vietnam Service ribbon.

The Army awards system has evolved into a highly structured program often called the *"Pyramid of Honor."* The system is designed to reward services ranging from heroism on the battlefield to superior performance of non combat duties.

Since World War II, the Army has generally embraced Napoleon's concept of liberally awarding medals and ribbons to enhance morale and esprit de corps. Over the years an expanded and specifically-tailored awards program became generally very popular in the all-volunteer Army and has played a significant part in improving morale, job performance, recruitment and reenlistments among junior officers and enlisted personnel.

The various ways of wearing decorations and awards by active duty, reserve and veterans are shown on the following pages. These awards paint a wonderful portrait of the American soldier whose dedication to the ideals of freedom represent the rich United States Army military heritage.

Ribbon Chart Showing the 1941 to 1974 U.S. Army Awards

The ribbon chart on page 96, reads left to right and shows the ribbon for every Army award from 1941 to 1974. The chart covers awards from World War II and the Korea War because some Vietnam veterans also served in those major conflicts. On page 98 are the Army's Unit Awards.

On page 97 the current correct order of precedence for Army ribbons is shown going back to World War II. Authorized attachments for each ribbon are displayed below the ribbon.

Next is the current Army Order of Precedence Chart for Unit Awards and directions for the wear of multi-service unit awards.

Army Ribbon Devices *(Appurtenances)* start on page 99 with examples of how to correctly mount ribbon devices on to ribbons and medals. Examples of mounting V devices, Oak Leaf clusters and Campaign Stars are shown.

Medals of America Press 5

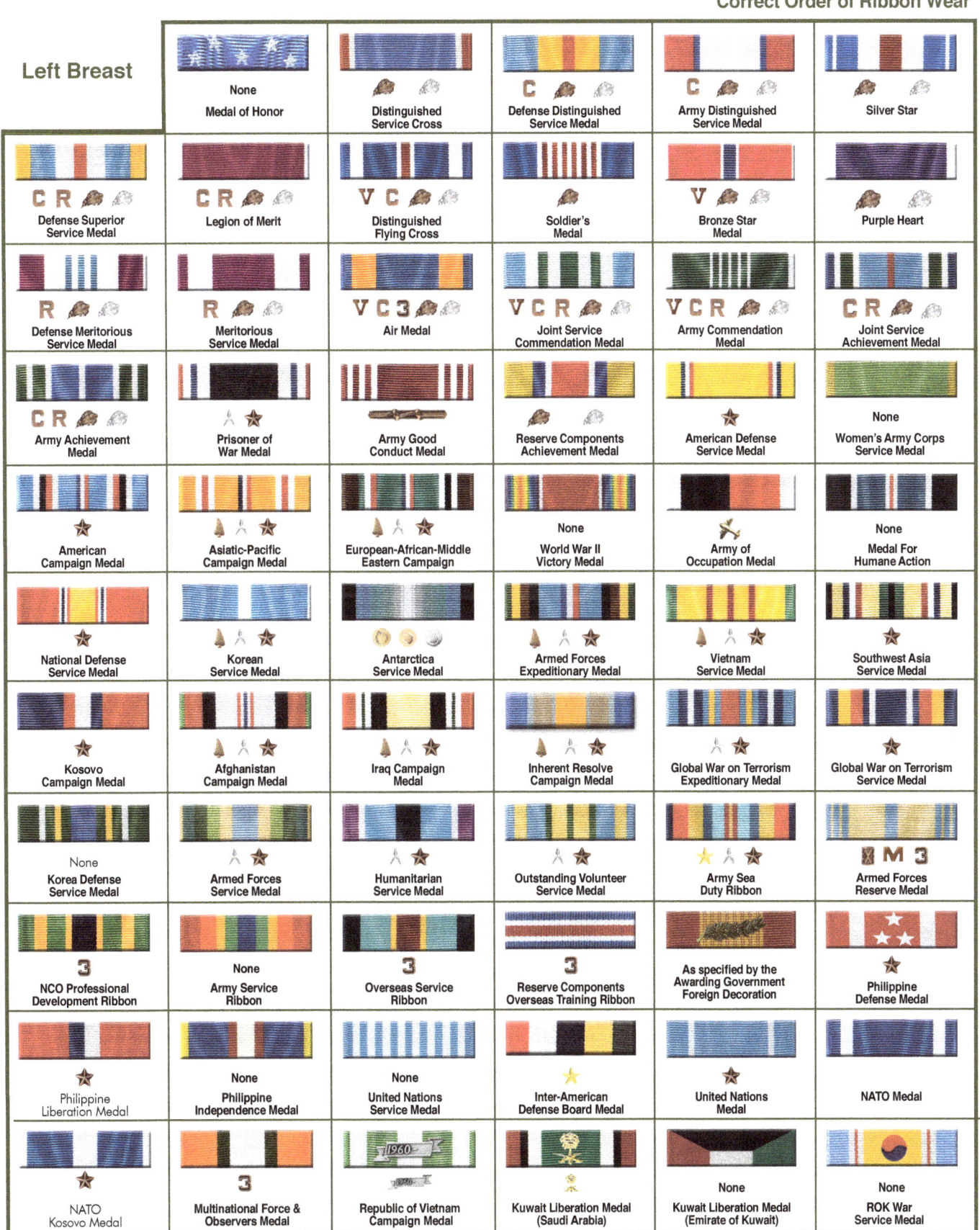

Army Unit Awards Today

Right Breast

Army Presidential Unit Citation

Joint Meritorious Unit Award

Army Valorous Unit Award

Army Meritorious Unit Commendation

Army Superior Unit Award not authorized until 1985

None
Philippine Presidential Unit Citation

None
Republic of Korea Presidential Unit Citation

None
Republic of Vietnam Presidential Unit Citation

Vietnam Gallantry Cross Unit Citation

Vietnam Civil Actions Unit Citation

Note: Per Army regulations, no row may contain more than four ribbons or three (3) unit awards. The display is arranged solely to conserve space on the page.

Wear of Multi-Service Unit Citations (Right Breast) on the U.S. Army Uniform

Personnel may wear U.S. and foreign unit award emblems on the service uniforms.

All permanent and temporary unit award emblems, with or without frames, are worn in the order of precedence from the wearer's right to left. Award emblems are worn in rows containing no more than three emblems per row, with no space between emblems, and with up to 1/8 inch space between rows, depending upon the size of emblems with frames. The emblems are worn as follows:

(1) **Male personnel.** Emblems with or without frames are worn centered with the bottom edge of the emblem 1/8 inch above the right breast pocket flap.

(2) **Female personnel.** Emblems with or without frames are worn centered on the right side of the uniform, with the bottom edge 1/2 inch above the top edge of the nameplate.

The following awards may not be worn on the Army uniform.

8 Medals, Badges and Insignia U.S. Army Vietnam

⭐ Placement of the Letter "V" on the Ribbon and Medal

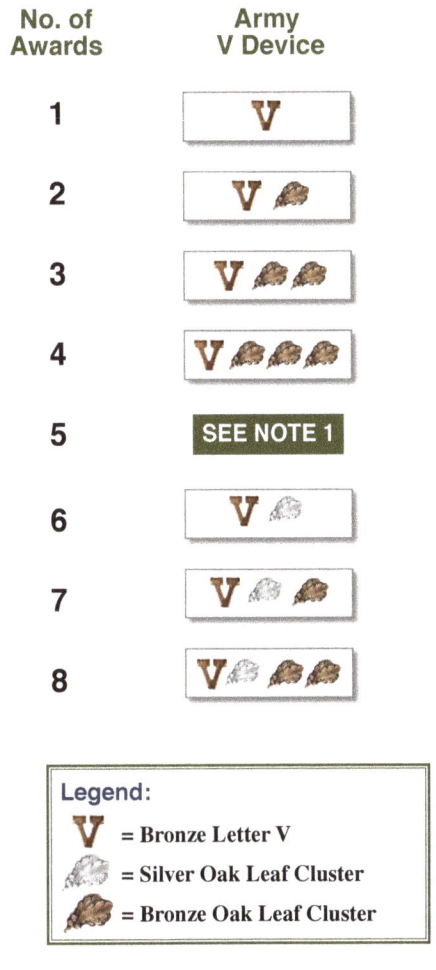

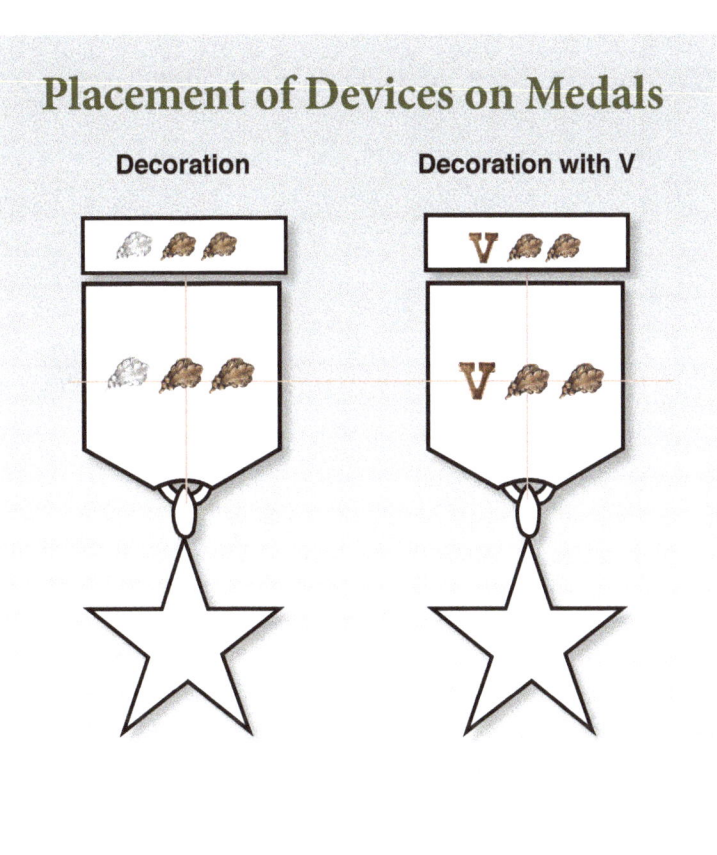

⭐ Placement of Oak Leaf Cluster Devices on the Ribbon

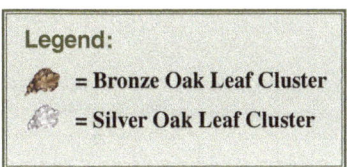

NOTE 1

1. Army and Air Force regulations limit the number of devices which may be worn on a single ribbon to a maximum of four (4). If more than four devices are authorized, a second ribbon is worn containing the excess devices.

Legend:
- 🍂 = Bronze Oak Leaf Cluster
- 🍂 = Silver Oak Leaf Cluster

⭐ Placement of Campaign Stars on the Ribbon

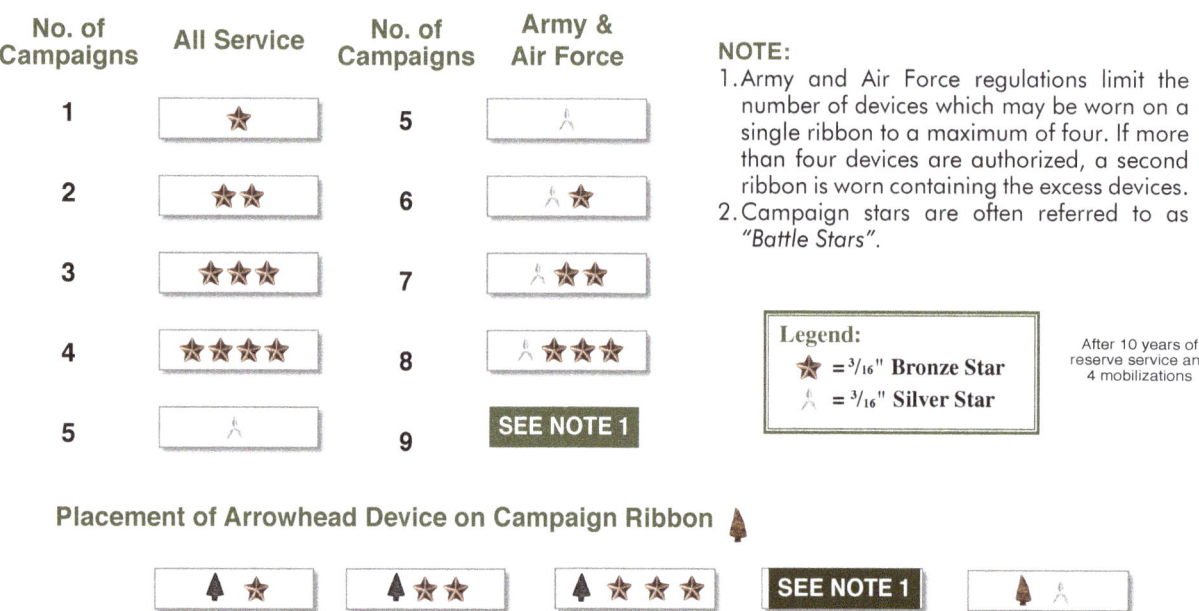

NOTE:
1. Army and Air Force regulations limit the number of devices which may be worn on a single ribbon to a maximum of four. If more than four devices are authorized, a second ribbon is worn containing the excess devices.
2. Campaign stars are often referred to as *"Battle Stars"*.

Legend:
⭐ = 3/16" **Bronze Star**
⚜ = 3/16" **Silver Star**

After 10 years of reserve service and 4 mobilizations

Placement of Arrowhead Device on Campaign Ribbon

President Johnson presents a Decoration In Vietnam

Medals, Badges and Insignia U.S. Army Vietnam

⭐ The United States Army Pyramid of Honor

The Pyramid of Honor

As mentioned earlier, the Army award system has evolved into a highly structured program which is called the *"Pyramid of Honor."* The system is designed to reward services ranging from heroism on the battlefield to superior performance of noncombatant duties and even includes the completion of entry level basic training.

Since World War II the Army has generally embraced Napoleon's concept of liberally awarding medals and ribbons to enhance morale and esprit de corps. The large number of Air Medals awarded in World War II is an example of this policy. Army Air Force losses were second only to the Infantry and the leadership wanted an immediate way to recognize the extraordinary service of the air crews. Over the years an expanded and specifically-tailored awards program became generally very popular in the all-volunteer Army and has played a significant part in improving morale, job performance, recruitment and reenlistments among junior officers and enlisted personnel.

On the next page is a chart showing all United States Military Medals for the six services; Army, Navy, Marines, Air Force, Coast Guard and Space Force. Some of these decorations and medals apply to all branches of the Armed Forces others just apply to the Army or Naval forces or the Air Force.

The decorations and awards which apply specifically to the Army and represent the rich United States Army military heritage are presented on the following pages. The details of these awards tell the story of the dedication to the ideals of freedom and sacrifices required to earn them.

The color plates display each medal and describe the service or services to which the award is authorized, the date instituted and the criteria for award along with appropriate attachments and in some cases examples of how they were earned.

The medals and ribbons are presented in the Army order of precedence beginning with the Medal of Honor and ending with the commonly awarded foreign medals and ribbons. The foreign section also includes an expanded area on the awards which may have been received by Army personnel from the Republic of South Vietnam.

The Army issues and presents all decorations and many of the service medals. With the exception of the Medal of Honor all of the medals and ribbons presented in this book can be purchased by veterans, their family, active-duty, Guard and Reserve. *However, make no mistake, it is against the law to buy or sell a United States Medal of Honor.*

The Stolen Valor Act

The Stolen Valor Act of 2005, was a statute that addressed the unauthorized wear, manufacture or sale of certain military decorations and medals. The law made it a federal misdemeanor to falsely represent oneself as having received any U.S. military decoration or medal. In United States v. Alvarez the U.S. Supreme Court ruled in 2012, that the Stolen Valor Act was too restrictive. In 2013, a new bill was introduced in Congress and the Stolen Valor Act of 2013 was signed into law by the President on 3 June, 2013.

The Medal of Honor

The Congressional Medal of Honor *(referred to universally as the Medal of Honor in all statutes, awards and uniform regulations)* was born in conflict and steeped in controversy during its early years until emerging as one of the world's premier awards for bravery.

Although there are three separate medals representing America's highest reward for bravery, there is only a single set of directives governing the award of the most coveted of all U.S. decorations.

Many Americans are confused by the term: *"Congressional Medal of Honor"* when, in fact, the proper term is *"Medal of Honor"*. Most confusion comes from a July 1918 law that authorizes the President to present the medal " … in the name of Congress".

In the United States, a totally democratic society, it is fitting that the first medal to reward valor on the battlefield should be for private soldiers and seamen *(later extended to officers)*.

The fact that all Medals of Honor recipients belong to the Congressional Medal of Honor Society, an official organization chartered by Congress, adds to the confusion. The medal is referred to universally as the *"Medal of Honor"*.

★ Army Medals of Honor

Ribbon

Rosette

The Army Medal of Honor was first awarded in 1862 but, owing to extensive copying by veterans groups, was redesigned in 1904 and patented by the War Department to ensure the design exclusivity.

The present medal, a five pointed golden star, lays over a green enamelled laurel wreath. The center of the star depicts Minerva, goddess of righteous war and wisdom, encircled by the words: *"United States of America"*.

The back of the medal is inscribed, *"The Congress to"*, with a place for the recipient's name. The medal hangs from a bar inscribed: *"Valor"*, which is held by an American eagle with laurel leaves *(denoting peace)* in its right talon and arrows *(war)* in its left. The eagle is fastened by a hook to a light blue silk pad on which are embroidered 13 stars.

Medals of America Press 13

Establishing Authority: The Army Medal of Honor was established by Joint Resolution of Congress, July 12, 1862 *(as amended)*

Effective Date: April 15, 1861

Criteria: Awarded for conspicuous gallantry and intrepidity at the risk of one's own life, above and beyond the call of duty. This gallantry must be performed either while engaged in action against an enemy of the United States, while engaged in military operations involving conflict with an opposing foreign force or while serving with friendly foreign forces engaged in an armed conflict against an opposing armed force in which the United States is not a belligerent party. Recommendation must be submitted within three years of the act and the medal must be awarded within five years of the act.

The current Army Medal of Honor was designed by the firm of Arthus Bertrand, Beranger & Magdelaine of Paris, France and is based on the original design of the Medal of Honor created in 1862 by William Wilson & Son Company of Philadelphia, Pennsylvania.

The Medal of Honor is a five-pointed gold-finished star (point down) with each point ending in a trefoil. Every point of the star has a green enamel oak leaf in its center and a green enamel laurel wreath surrounds the center of the star, passing just below the trefoils. In the center of the star is a profile of the Goddess Minerva encircled by the inscription, *"UNITED STATES OF AMERICA"*, with a small shield at the bottom. The star is suspended by links from a bar inscribed, *"VALOR"*, topped by a spread winged eagle grasping laurel leaves in its right talon and arrows in the left. The star represents each State in the United States. The oak leaf represents strength and the laurel leaf represents achievement. The head of Minerva represents wisdom with the shield from the Great Seal of the United States representing lawful authority. The laurel leaves clasped in the right claw of the Federal eagle offer peace while the arrows represent military might if the country's offer of peace is rejected. The back of the bar holding the star is engraved, *"THE CONGRESS TO."* The rest of the medal is smooth to permit engraving the recipient's name. The ribbon is a light blue moiré patterned silk neck band one and three sixteenths inches wide and twenty four inches long, with a square pad in the center of the same ribbon. Thirteen white stars are woven into the pad.

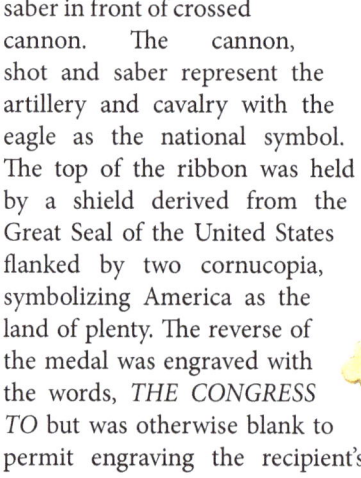

saber in front of crossed cannon. The cannon, shot and saber represent the artillery and cavalry with the eagle as the national symbol. The top of the ribbon was held by a shield derived from the Great Seal of the United States flanked by two cornucopia, symbolizing America as the land of plenty. The reverse of the medal was engraved with the words, *THE CONGRESS TO* but was otherwise blank to permit engraving the recipient's name.

Army Medal of Honor
(May 2, 1896 to April 23, 1904)

In the years following the Civil War, many veteran's organizations and other patriotic societies adopted membership badges and insignia which were thinly-disguised replicas of the Medal of Honor. To protect the sanctity of the Medal of Honor, Congress authorized a new ribbon for the Army Medal of Honor in 1896 to clearly distinguish it from veterans association's badges. The basic colors of the original ribbon were not changed, but simply altered.

Army Medal of Honor
(April 23, 1904 to 1944)

Unfortunately, the Army Medal of Honor continued to be widely copied and its design criticized. On April 23, 1904 a new design was approved and was granted Patent Number 197,369. In addition to the new planchet, the redesigned award was suspended from the now familiar light blue moire ribbon symbolic of the loyalty and vigilance, containing 13 embroidered white stars representing the 13 original states. This new version of the Medal of Honor is the design that is still used to the present day.

The only change that has taken place since its adoption in 1904 is the suspension which was modified in 1942 from a pin on breast ribbon to a neck ribbon.

Army Medal of Honor
(July 12, 1862 to May 1, 1896)

The first Army Medal of Honor had the same five-pointed star and flag ribbon as the Navy. The only differences were in the means of suspension. While the Navy medal was suspended by a fouled anchor, the Army's was suspended from an American eagle with outstretched wings with a stack of eight cannon balls and a

⭐ Distinguished Service Cross

Authorized by Congress on July 9, 1918. Awarded for extraordinary heroism against an armed enemy but of a level not justifying the award of the Medal of Honor. It may be awarded to both civilians and military serving in any capacity with the Army who distinguish themselves by heroic actions in combat. The act or acts of heroism must be so notable and have involved risk of life so extraordinary as to set the individual apart from his comrades. The medal had been initially proposed for award to qualifying members of the American Expeditionary Forces in Europe during World War I but was authorized permanently by Congress in the Appropriations Act of 1918. The Cross was designed by 1st Lt. Andre Smith and Captain Aymar Embury with the final design sculpted by John R. Sinnock at the Philadelphia Mint.

While DSCs were originally numbered, the practice was discontinued during World War II. In 1934 the DSC was authorized to be presented to holders of the Certificate of Merit which had been discontinued in 1918 when the Distinguished Service Medal was established. The medal is a cross with an eagle with spread wings centered on the cross behind which is a circular wreath of laurel leaves. The cross has decorative fluted edges with a small ornamental scroll topped by a ball at the end of each arm. The laurel wreath is tied at its base by a scroll which upon which are written the words, *"FOR VALOR."* The eagle represents the United States and the laurel leaves surrounding the eagle representing victory and achievement.

Service: Army
Instituted: 1918
Criteria: Extraordinary heroism in action against an enemy of the U.S. while engaged in military operations involving conflict with an opposing foreign force or while serving with friendly foreign forces.
Devices:

The reverse of the cross features the same decorations at the edges that appear on the front. The eagle's wings, back and tips also show. Centered on the reverse of the cross is a laurel wreath. In the center of the wreath is a decorative rectangular plaque for engraving the soldier's name. The ribbon has a one inch wide center of national blue edged in white and red. The national colors taken from the flag stand for sacrifice (red), purity *(white)* and high purpose *(blue)*.

⭐ Defense Distinguished Service Medal

Authorized on July 9, 1970 and awarded to military officers for exceptionally meritorious service while assigned to a Department of Defense joint activity. The Secretary of Defense is the awarding authority for the medal and it is usually only awarded to very senior officers. Examples of assignments that may allow qualification for this medal are: Chairman, Joint Chiefs of Staff; Chiefs and Vice Chiefs of the Military Services, including the Commandant and Assistant Commandant of the Marine Corps and Commanders and Vice Commanders of Unified and Specified Commands. It may also be awarded to other senior officers who serve in positions of great responsibility or to an officer whose direct and individual contributions to national security or defense are also recognized as being so exceptional in scope and value as to be equivalent to contributions normally associated with positions encompassing broader responsibilities. Subsequent awards are denoted by bronze and silver oak leaf clusters.

The medal depicts an American bald eagle with wings spread and the United States shield on its breast; the eagle is superimposed on a medium blue pentagon (which represents the five services) and is surrounded by a gold circle that has thirteen stars in the upper half and a laurel and olive wreath in the lower half. On the reverse of the medal is the inscription, *"FOR DISTINGUISHED SERVICE... FROM THE SECRETARY OF DEFENSE TO"* space is provided below the TO for engraving of the recipient's name. The ribbon has

Service: All
Instituted: 1970
Criteria: Exceptionally meritorious service to the United States while assigned to a Joint Activity in a position of unique and great responsibility.
Devices:

a central stripe of red flanked by stripes of gold and blue. The red represents zeal and courageous action, the gold denotes excellence and the medium blue represents the Department of Defense.

The Defense Distinguished Service Medal was designed by Mildred Orloff and sculpted by Lewis J. King, Jr., both of the Institute of Heraldry.

⭐ Distinguished Service Medal *(Army)*

Authorized by Congress on July 9, 1918 for exceptionally meritorious service to the United States while serving in a duty of great responsibility with the U.S. Army. It was originally intended for qualifying actions during wartime only but was later authorized during both wartime or peacetime. As this country's highest award for meritorious service or achievement, it has been awarded to both military and civilians, foreign and domestic. The first American to receive this medal on October 12, 1918 was General John J. Pershing, Commanding General of the American Expeditionary Forces during World War I. Individuals who had received the Certificate of Merit before its disestablishment in 1918 were authorized to receive the DSM. The Army DSM is seldom awarded to civilians and personnel below the rank of Brigadier General.

The medal is a circular design containing the U.S. Coat of Arms encircled by a blue ring with the inscription, *"FOR DISTINGUISHED SERVICE MCMXVII"*. Subsequent awards are denoted by the attachment of a bronze oak leaf cluster to the medal and ribbon. In the center of the reverse of the medal, amidst several flags and weapons, is a blank scroll for engraving the awardees name.

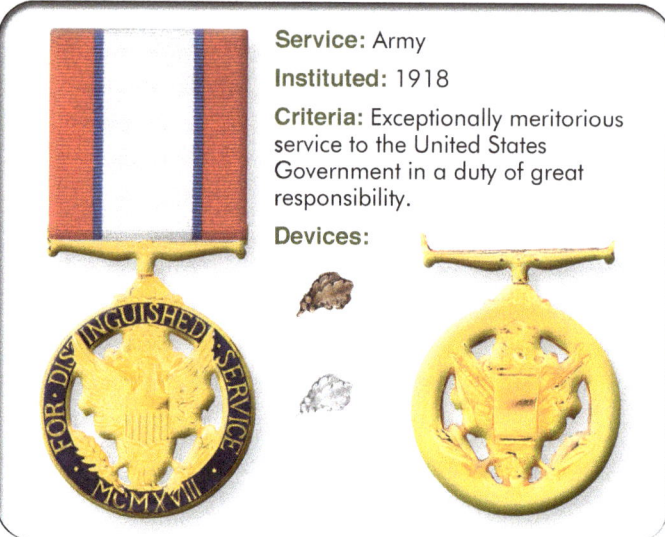

Service: Army
Instituted: 1918
Criteria: Exceptionally meritorious service to the United States Government in a duty of great responsibility.
Devices:

The ribbon has a central wide white stripe edged with blue and an outer red band representing the colors of the U.S. flag. The Army Distinguished Service Medal was designed by Captain Aymar E. Embury III and sculpted by Private Gaetano Cecere.

⭐ Silver Star

Awarded for gallantry in action against an enemy of the United States or while engaged in military operations involving conflict against an opposing armed force in which the United States is not a belligerent party. The level of gallantry required, while of a high degree, is less than that required for the Medal of Honor, Distinguished Service Cross. The Silver Star is derived from the Army's *"Citation Star"*, a 3/16" dia. silver star device which was worn on the ribbon bar and suspension ribbon of the *"appropriate Army campaign medal"* by any soldier cited in orders for gallantry in action. Although most applicable to the World War I Victory Medal, it was retroactive to all Army campaign medals dating back to the Civil War.

The actual Silver Star Medal was instituted in 1932 with the first award presented to General Douglas MacArthur, the Army's then-Chief-of-Staff. The Silver Star was designed by Rudolf Freund of the firm of Bailey, Banks and Biddle. On August 7, 1942, the award was extended to Navy personnel and, later that year, authorized for civilians serving with the armed forces who met the stated criteria specified in the initial regulation.

The medal is a five-pointed star finished in gilt-bronze. In the center of the star is a three-sixteenths inch silver five-pointed star within a wreath of laurel, representing the silver [citation] star prescribed by the original legislation. The rays of both stars align. The top of the medal has a rectangular-shaped loop for the suspension ribbon. The laurel wreath signifies achievement and the larger gilt-bronze star represents military service. The reverse

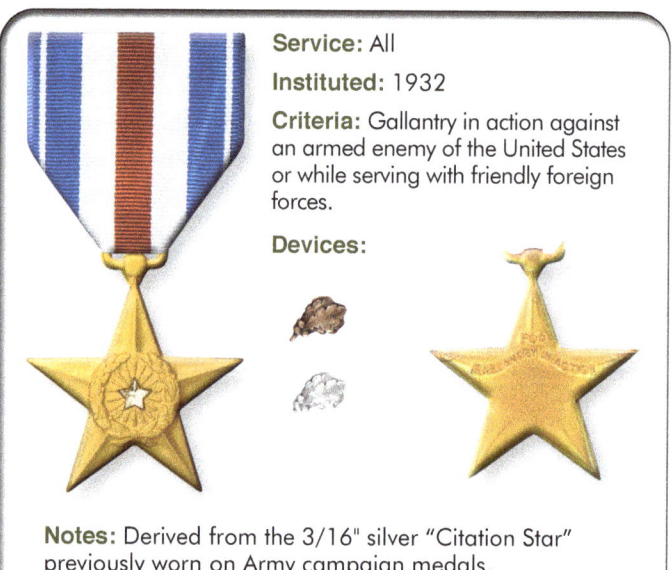

Service: All
Instituted: 1932
Criteria: Gallantry in action against an armed enemy of the United States or while serving with friendly foreign forces.
Devices:

Notes: Derived from the 3/16" silver "Citation Star" previously worn on Army campaign medals.

contains the inscription, *"FOR GALLANTRY IN ACTION"* with a space to engrave the name of the recipient.

The ribbon, based on the colors of the National flag, has a center stripe of red flanked by a stripes of white which are flanked by blue bands with borders of white edged in blue. Additional awards are denoted by a bronze or silver oak leaf clusters.

Legion of Merit

Bronze   Anodized or Gold-Plated

Medal Reverse

Authorized by Congress on July 20, 1942 for award to members of the Armed Forces of the United States for exceptionally meritorious conduct in the performance of outstanding service. Superior performance of normal duties will not alone justify award of this decoration. It is not awarded for heroism but rather for service and achievement while performing duties in a key position of responsibility. It may be presented to foreign personnel but is not authorized for presentation to civilian personnel. There are four degrees of this decoration that are awarded to foreign personnel only (*Chief Commander, Commander, Officer and Legionnaire*). The first two degrees are comparable in rank to the Distinguished Service Medal and are usually awarded to heads of state and to commanders of armed forces, respectively. The last two degrees are comparable in rank to the award of the Legion of Merit to U.S. service members. The Medal was designed by Colonel Robert Townsend Heard and sculpted by Katharine W. Lane.

The name and design of the Legion of Merit was strongly influenced by the French Legion of Honor. The medal is a white enameled five-armed cross with ten points, each tipped with a gold ball and bordered in red enamel. In the center of the cross, thirteen stars on a blue field are surrounded by a circle of heraldic clouds. A green enameled laurel wreath circles behind the arms of the cross. Between the wreath and the center of the medal and in between the arms of the cross are two crossed arrows pointing outward. The blue circle with thirteen stars surrounded by clouds is taken from the Great Seal of the United States and is symbolic of a *"new constellation,"* as the signers of the Declaration of Independence called our new republic. The laurel wreath represents achievement, while the arrows represent protection of the nation. The reverse of the cross is a gold colored copy of the front with blank space to be used for engraving The raised inscription, *"ANNUIT COEPTIS MDCCLXXXII"* with a bullet separating each word encircles the area to be engraved. The words, *"UNITED STATES OF AMERICA"* and *"ANNUIT COEPTIS"* (He [God] Has Favored Our Undertaking) come from the Great Seal of the United States and the date, *"MDCCLXXXII"* (1782) refers to the year General Washington established the Badge of Military Merit. The ribbon is a purple-red called American Beauty Red which is edged in white. The color is a variation of the original color of the Badge of Military Merit.

Service	All Services
Instituted	1942 *(retroactive to 8 Sept 1939)*
Criteria	Exceptionally meritorious conduct in the performance of outstanding services to the United States.
Devices	Bronze, Silver Oak Leaf Cluster; Letter "V" *(for valor)* not authorized
Notes	Issued in four degrees *(Legionnaire, Officer, Commander & Chief Commander)* to foreign nationals.

President Franklin D. Roosevelt, established the rules for the Legion of Merit and required the President's approval for the award. However, in 1943, at the request of General George C. Marshall, approval authority for U.S. personnel was delegated to the War Department.

Executive Order 10600, dated March 15, 1955, by President Dwight D. Eisenhower, revised approval authority. Current provisions are contained in Title 10, United States Code 1121.

Distinguished Flying Cross

Bronze   Anodized or Gold-Plated   Medal Reverse

Regulation Ribbon Bar

Enamel Lapel Pin

Miniature Medals

Mini Ribbon (unofficial)

Enamel Hat Pin (unofficial)

The Distinguished Flying Cross was authorized on July 2, 1926 and implemented by an executive order signed by President Calvin Coolidge on January 28, 1927. It is awarded to United States military personnel for heroism or extraordinary achievement that is clearly distinctive involving operations during aerial flight that are not routine. It is the first decoration authorized in identical design and ribbon to all branches of the U.S. Armed Forces. Captain Charles A. Lindbergh was the first recipient of the Distinguished Flying Cross for his solo flight across the Atlantic. The Wright Brothers were awarded the DFC by an Act of Congress for their first manned flight at Kitty Hawk, North Carolina in 1903. Amelia Earhart became the only female civilian to be awarded the DFC when it was presented to her by the United States Army Air Corps for her aerial exploits. Such awards to civilians were prohibited on March 1, 1927 by Executive Order 4601.

While the Distinguished Flying Cross was never intended to be an automatic award, the Army Air Force did use it in that capacity many times during World War II by awarding DFCs for specific number of sorties and flying hours in a combat theater.

The front of the medal is a four-bladed propeller contained within a bronze cross suspended from a straight bar attached to the medal drape. The reverse is blank and provides space for the recipient's name and date of the award. The ribbon is blue with a narrow stripe of red bordered by white in the center. The ribbon edges are outlined with bands of white inside blue. Additional awards are denoted by bronze and silver oak leaf clusters or gold and silver stars depending on the recipient's Service Branch.

Service	All Services
Instituted	1926 (retroactive to 6 April 1917)
Criteria	Heroism or extraordinary achievement while participating in aerial flight.
Devices	Letter "V" Devices: Bronze, Silver Oak Leaf Cluster

This display of a Vietnam Warrant Officer Pilot shows his awards of the Distinguished Flying Cross, Bronze Star, Purple Heart Medal, Multiplie Air Medals, the Army Commendation Medal, National Defence Service Medal, the Vietnam Service Medal, the RVN Cross of Gallantry and the RVN Campaign Medal.

18   Medals, Badges and Insignia U.S. Army Vietnam

⭐ Soldier's Medal

Authorized by Congress on July 2, 1926 to any member of the Army, National Guard or Reserves for heroism not involving actual conflict with an armed enemy.

The bronze octagonal medal has, as its central feature, a North American bald eagle with raised wings representing the United States. The eagle grasps an ancient Roman fasces symbolizing the State's lawful authority and conveys the concept that the award is to a soldier from the Government. There are seven stars on the eagle's left side and six stars and a spray of leaves to its right. The octagonal shape distinguishes the Soldier's Medal from other decorations. The stars represent the thirteen original colonies that formed the United States. The laurel spray balances the groups of stars and represents achievement. The reverse has a U.S. shield with sprays of laurel and oak leaves representing achievement and strength in front of a scroll. The words, *"SOLDIER'S MEDAL"* and *"FOR VALOR"* are inscribed on the reverse.

The ribbon contains thirteen alternating stripes of white *(seven)* and red *(six)* in the center, bordered by blue and are taken from the United States flag. The thirteen red and white stripes are arranged in the same manner as the thirteen vertical stripes in the U.S. Coat of Arms shield and also represent the thirteen original colonies.

Service: Army
Instituted: 1926
Criteria: Heroism not involving actual conflict with an armed enemy of the United States.
Devices:

Gaetano Cecere designed and sculpted the Soldier's Medal *(the art deco influence of the 1920's can certainly be seen in this medal more than in any other Army award)*. The Soldier's Medal is one of four decorations for which an enlisted soldier may increase his retirement by ten percent. The increase is not automatic, however; recipients of the Soldier's Medal must petition the Army Decorations Board for the bonus. Additional awards are denoted by oak leaf clusters.

⭐ Bronze Star Medal

Bronze Star continued on the next page.

Medals of America Press 19

Bronze Star Medal

Bronze   Anodized or Gold-Plated   Medal Reverse

Regulation Ribbon Bar

Enamel Lapel Pin

Mini Ribbons (unofficial)

Miniature Medals

Enamel Hat Pin (unofficial)

Authorized on February 4, 1944, retroactive to December 7, 1941. It is awarded to individuals who, while serving in the United States Armed Forces in a combat theater, distinguish themselves by heroism, outstanding achievement or by meritorious service not involving aerial flight.

The Bronze Star was originally conceived by the U.S. Navy as a junior decoration comparable to the Air Medal for heroic or meritorious actions by ground and surface personnel. The level of required service would not be sufficient to warrant the Silver Star if awarded for heroism or the Legion of Merit if awarded for meritorious achievement. In a strange twist of fate, the Bronze Star Medal did not reach fruition until championed by General George C. Marshall, the Army Chief of Staff during World War II. Marshall was seeking a decoration that would reward front line troops, particularly infantrymen, whose ranks suffered the heaviest casualties and were forced to endure the greatest danger and hardships during the conflict. Once established, the Bronze Star Medal virtually became the sole province of the Army in terms of the number of medals awarded.

Although Marshall wanted the Bronze Star Medal to be awarded with the same freedom as the Air Medal, it never came close to the vast numbers of Air Medals distributed during the war. The only exception was the award of the Bronze Star Medal to every soldier of the 101st Airborne Division who had fought in the Normandy invasion, Operation Market Garden in Holland, the Battle of the Bulge or were wounded.

After the war, when the ratio of Air Medals awarded to airmen was compared to the numbers of Bronze Star Medals awarded to combat soldiers, it became clear that a huge disparity existed and many troops who deserved the award for their service had not received it. Therefore, in September 1947, the Bronze Star Medal was authorized for all personnel who had received either the Combat Infantryman's Badge *(CIB)* or the Combat Medical Badge *(CMB)* between December 7, 1941 to September 2, 1945. In addition, personnel who had participated in the defense of the Philippine Islands between December 7, 1941 and May 10, 1942 were awarded the Bronze Star Medal if their service was on the island of Luzon, the Bataan Peninsula or the harbor defenses on Corregidor Island and they had been awarded the Philippine Presidential Unit Citation.

Service	All Services
Instituted	1944 (retroactive to 7 Dec. 1941)
Criteria	The Bronze Star Medal is awarded to individuals who, while serving in the United States Armed Forces in a combat theater, distinguish themselves by heroism, outstanding achievement or by meritorious service not involving aerial flight.
Devices	Letter "V" *(for Valor)* Devices Army/Air Force: Bronze, Silver Oak Leaf Cluster.

The Bronze Star Medal is a five-pointed bronze star with a smaller star in the center *(similar in design to the Silver Star Medal);* the reverse contains the inscription, *"HEROIC OR MERITORIOUS ACHIEVEMENT"* in a circular pattern. The ribbon is red with a white-edged blue band in the center and white edge stripes. The Bronze Star Medal was designed by Rudolf Freund of Bailey, Banks and Biddle.

Purple Heart

Bronze

Anodized or Gold-Plated

Regulation Ribbon Bar

Enamel Lapel Pin

Medal Reverse

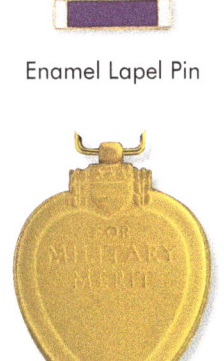
Enamel Hat Pin
(unofficial)

Mini Ribbon
(unofficial)

Miniature Medals

The Purple Heart is America's oldest military decoration. It was originally established on August 7, 1782 by General George Washington who designed the original award called the *"Badge of Military Merit."* The Badge of Military Merit was awarded for singularly meritorious action to a deserving hero of the Revolutionary War. There were only three known recipients of the award, all of whom were noncommissioned officers of the Continental Army. The Badge of Military Merit was intended by Washington to be a permanent decoration but was never used again after the three initial presentations until it was reestablished as the Purple Heart Medal on February 22, 1932 *(the 200th anniversary of Washington's birth)* by the Army War Department.

During the First World War, War Department General Order No.134 of October 12, 1917 authorized a red ribbon with a narrow white center stripe to be worn on the right breast for wounds received in action. However, the order was rescinded 32 days later and the ribbon never became a reality. Instead the Army authorized wound chevrons which were worn on the lower right sleeve of the tunic.

On July 21, 1932, General Douglas MacArthur, who was a key figure in its revival, received the first Purple Heart after it was reestablished. President Franklin D. Roosevelt signed an executive order on December 3, 1942 that expanded the award to members of the Navy, Marine Corps and Coast Guard as well. Although the Purple Heart was awarded for meritorious service between 1932 and 1943, the primary purpose of the award has always been to recognize those who received wounds while in military service.

Service	All Services *(Originally Army Only)* 
Instituted	1932; The Purple Heart is retroactive to 5 April 1917; however, awards for qualifying prior to that date have been made.
Criteria	Awarded to any member of the Armed Forces of the United States or to any civilian national of the United States who, while serving under competent authority in any capacity with one of the U.S. Armed Forces, since 5 April 1917 has been wounded, killed, or who has died or may die of wounds received from an opposing enemy force while in armed combat or as a result of an act of international terrorism or being a Prisoner of War.
Devices	Bronze, Silver Oak Leaf Cluster

Later Presidential Executive Orders extended eligibility for the Purple Heart to military and civilian personnel who received wounds from a terrorist attack or while performing peace keeping duties. Currently, it is awarded for wounds received while serving in any capacity with one of the U.S. Armed Forces after April 5, 1917; it may be awarded to civilians as well as military personnel. The wounds may have been received while in combat against an enemy, while a member of a peacekeeping force, while a Prisoner of War, as a result of a terrorist attack or as a result of a friendly fire incident in hostile territory. The 1996 Defense Authorization Act extended eligibility for the Purple Heart to prisoners of war before 25 April 1962; 1962 legislation had only authorized the medal to POWs after 25 April 1962. Wounds that qualify must have required treatment by a medical officer or must be a matter of official record.

The Purple Heart was designed by the Army's Institute of Heraldry from a design originally submitted by General Douglas MacArthur and modeled by John Sinnock, Chief Engraver at the Philadelphia Mint. The medal is a purple heart with a bronze gilt border and a bronze profile of George Washington in the center. Above the heart is a shield from George Washington's Coat of Arms between two sprays of green enameled leaves. On the back of the medal, below the Coat of Arms and leaves, there is a raised bronze heart with the raised inscription *FOR MILITARY MERIT* and room to inscribe the name of the recipient. Initially the medals were numbered, but this practice was discontinued in July 1943 as a cost-cutting measure. The ribbon is purple edged in white. Additional awards are denoted by Bronze and Silver Oak Leaf clusters.

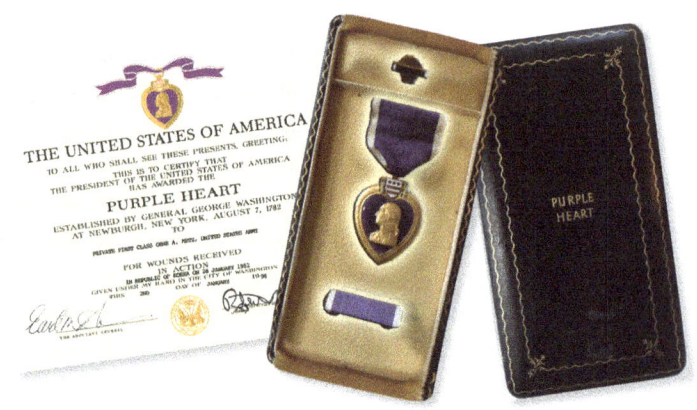

World War II Purple Heart Presentation Case

Early Purple Hearts were numbered on the edge of the medal.

The World War II Purple Hearts are generally identified by the high quality of workmanship and a single white stitch under the left and right edge of the ribbon bar of the medal drape. It is not improbable for a Vietnam veteran to receive the Purple Heart Medal that was originally manufactured for his grandfather's generation.

Purple Heart License Plate

Purple Heart Stamp

The Purple Heart Medal has always been highly respected by military personnel since it was earned by giving one's life or being wounded while in military service of our country. Shown above is a World War II Purple Heart and its WW II period presentation box. The presentation came with the medal, a ribbon and a lapel pin. During World War II contracts were issued for over a million and a half Purple Heart medals with the largest number being produced in anticipation of the invasion of Japan.

The Japanese Armed Forces determination to fight to the death during the Pacific campaign led everyone, especially the Navy and Marines to anticipate heavy casualties. The government requested so many Purple Hearts be manufactured that it was not until almost 1947 that all the contracts were completed. Meanwhile the Air Force bombing campaign and the use of the first atomic bombs lead to the capitulation of Japan and ended the requirement for the huge order of Purple Heart Medals.

Approximately a half million Purple Hearts went into the military inventories after World War II. Even with many of these medals presented during the Korean and Vietnam eras there were over 100,000 World War II Purple Heart medals still in the military supply chain during the Vietnam . Refurbished, many of these Purple Hearts continued to be awarded to veterans.

Vietnam Veteran's awards with the Purple Heart Medal

Vietnam Veteran's awards with the Purple Heart Medal

⭐ Meritorious Service Medal

Authorized on January 16, 1969 and awarded to members of the Armed Forces for noncombat meritorious achievement or meritorious service after that date. The Meritorious Service Medal evolved from an initial recommendation in 1918 by General John J. Pershing, the Commander of the American Expeditionary Forces during World War I. He suggested that an award for meritorious service be created to provide special recognition to deserving individuals by the U.S. government. Although the request by General Pershing was disapproved, it was revisited several more times during World War II and afterwards. During the Vietnam War the proposal to create the medal received significant attention and was eventually approved when President Lyndon B. Johnson signed the executive order on January 16, 1969. The Meritorious Service Medal cannot be awarded for service in a combat theater. It has often been the decoration of choice for both end of tour and retirement recognition for field grade officers and senior enlisted personnel.

The MSM is a bronze medal with six rays rising from the top of a five-pointed star with beveled edges with two smaller stars outlined within. On the lower part of the medal in front of the star there is an eagle with its wings spread. It is standing on two curving laurel branches tied between the eagle's talons. The eagle, symbol of the nation, holds laurel branches representing achievement. The star represents military service with the rays symbolizing individual efforts to achieve excellence. The reverse of the medal has the inscription, *"UNITED STATES OF AMERICA"* at the top and *"MERITORIOUS SERVICE"* at

Service: All Services
Instituted: 1969
Criteria: Outstanding noncombat meritorious achievement or service to the United States.
Devices:

the bottom; the space inside the circle formed by the text is to be used for engraving the recipient's name. The ribbon is ruby red with two white stripes and is a variation of the Legion of Merit ribbon. Jay Morris and Lewis J. King of the Institute of Heraldry designed and sculpted the Meritorious Service Medal. Additional awards are indicated by bronze and silver oak leaf clusters on the recipient's Service Branch.

⭐ Air Medal

Authorized on May 11, 1942. Awarded for single acts of achievement after September 8, 1939, to individuals who distinguish themselves by heroism, outstanding achievement or by meritorious service while participating in aerial flight. In WW II the Air Medal was to be awarded for a lesser degree of heroism or achievement than required for the DFC. Many AAF units began to award the Air Medal on a quota basis, e.g. 20 missions equaled one Air Medal or an Air Medal for every enemy aircraft shot down. Some commands carried this to extremes by awarding a DFC for every 5 Air Medals. By the end of WW II, over a million Air Medals were awarded *(many of which were, of course, oak leaf clusters)*. While some will say this was extreme, in truth the generous award of the Air Medal provided combat aircrews a visible sign that their devotion and determination were appreciated by the country. The Air Medal helped keep morale up in a force that suffered the highest casualty rate of the war after the Infantry. The Bronze Star was meant to be the equivalent of the Air Medal for the infantry but it was not until after WW II that it was awarded in bulk to honor combat infantry and medics.

The Army Air Force used oak leaf clusters to indicate additional awards while the Army has used numerals since 1968.

The Air Medal was often awarded in Vietnam to combat arms soldiers for a certain number of helicopter assaults and Army helicopter pilots were often awarded numerous air medals reflecting their huge number of combat missions. The medal is a bronze sixteen point compass rose suspended by a Fleur-de-lis. In the center there is an diving eagle carrying a lighting bolt in each talon. The compass rose represents the global capacity of American air power. The lightning bolts show the United States' ability to wage war from the air. The Fleur-de-lis represents the high ideals of American airmen. The reverse of the compass rose is plain with an area for engraving the recipient's name. The ribbon is ultramarine blue with two golden orange stripes representing the colors of the Army Air Force. The Air Medal was designed and sculpted by Walker Hancock.

Service	All Services
Instituted	1942 *(Retroactive to 8 September 1939)*
Criteria	Heroic actions or meritorious service while participating in aerial flight, but not of a degree that would justify an award of the Distinguished Flying Cross.
Devices	Bronze, Silver Oak Leaf, Bronze "V", Numerals
Notes	During World War II, the Army Air Corps and U.S. Army Air Force employed bronze and silver oak leaf clusters as additional award devices on all decorations including the Air Medal. The same devices were used by the Army until the establishment of the bronze numeral in 1967 as its unique additional award device for the Air Medal during the Vietnam War.

24 Medals, Badges and Insignia U.S. Army Vietnam

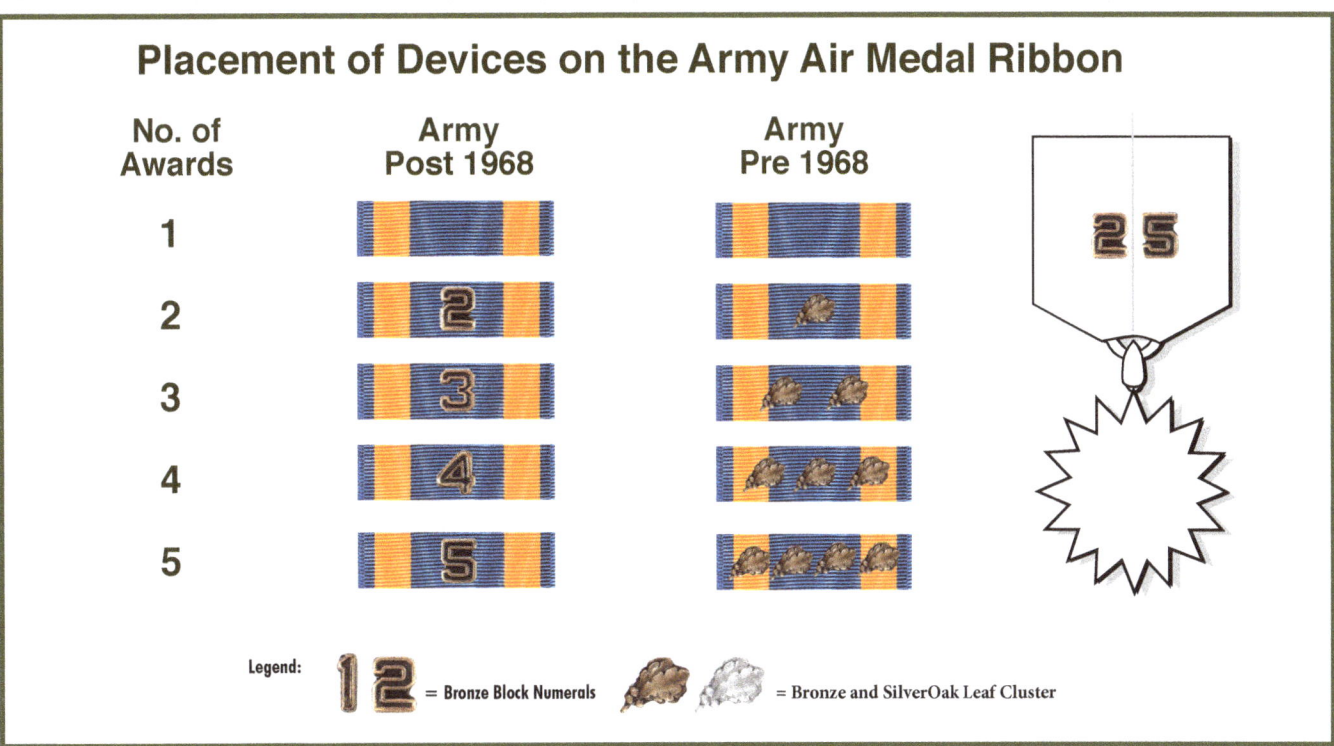

Placement of Devices on the Army Air Medal Ribbon

No. of Awards	Army Post 1968	Army Pre 1968
1		
2		
3		
4		
5		

Legend: **1 2** = Bronze Block Numerals   = Bronze and Silver Oak Leaf Cluster

Medals of America Press

Joint Service Commendation Medal

Authorized on June 25, 1963, this was the first medal specifically authorized for members of a Joint Service organization. Awarded to members of the Armed Forces for meritorious achievement or service while serving in a Joint Activity after January 1, 1963. The "V" device is authorized if the award is made for direct participation in combat operations between 15 June, 1963 and 31 March 1976.

Service: All Services (by Secretary of Defense)
Instituted: 1963
Criteria: Meritorious service or achievement while assigned to a Joint Activity.
Devices:

The medal consists of four conjoined green enameled hexagons edged in gold which represent the unity of the Armed Forces. The top hexagon has thirteen gold five-pointed stars (representing the thirteen original states) and the lower hexagon has a gold stylized heraldic device *(for land, air and sea)*. An eagle with spread wings and a shield on its breast is in the center of the hexagons. The eagle is grasping three arrows in its talons. The hexagons are encircled by a laurel wreath bound with gold bands (representing achievement). On the reverse there is a plaque for engraving the recipient's name. Above the plaque are the raised words, *"FOR MILITARY"* and below, *"MERIT"* with a laurel spray below. The words and laurel spray are derived from the Army and Navy Commendation Medals. The ribbon is a center stripe of green flanked by white, green, white and light blue stripes. The green and white are from the Army and Navy Commendation ribbons and the light blue represents the Department of Defense. Oak leaf clusters denote additional awards.

Army Commendation Medal

Authorized on December 18, 1945 as a commendation ribbon and awarded to members of the Army for heroism, meritorious achievement or meritorious service after December 6, 1941. It was meant for award where the Bronze Star Medal was not appropriate, i.e., outside of operational areas.

Service: Army
Instituted: 1945 *(retroactive to 1941)*
Criteria: Heroism, meritorious achievement or meritorious service.
Devices:

The Army Commendation Medal, commonly called the ARCOM, is unique as it is the first and only Army award that started as a ribbon-only award and then became a medal. After World War II, it became the only award created for the express purpose of peacetime and wartime meritorious service as well as the only award designed expressly for presentation to junior officers and enlisted personnel. In short, the *ARCOM* became the peacetime version of the Bronze Star Medal to recognize outstanding performance and boost morale. Subsequent to World War II, retroactive awards of the Commendation Ribbon were authorized for any individual who had received a Letter of Commendation from a Major General or higher before January 1, 1946.

In 1947, the rules were changed allowing the *ARCOM* to be awarded in connection with military operations for which the level of service did not meet the requirements for the Bronze Star or Air Medal. In 1949 the change from a ribbon-only award to a pendant was approved. Anyone who received the ribbon could apply for the new medal. The Army redesignated the Commendation Ribbon With Metal Pendant as the Army Commendation Medal in 1960. In 1962, it was authorized for award to a member of the Armed Forces of a friendly nation for the same level of achievement or service which was mutually beneficial to that nation and the United States. The next big change occurred on February 29, 1964 with the approval of the "V" device to denote combat heroism of a degree less than that required for the Bronze Star Medal. Additionally, the ARCOM continued to be awarded for acts of courage not qualifying for the Soldier's Medal.

The medal, a bronze hexagon, depicts the American bald eagle with spread wings on the face. The eagle has the U.S. shield on its breast and is grasping three crossed arrows in its talons. On the reverse of the medal are inscriptions *"FOR MILITARY"* and with a plaque for engraving the recipient's name between the two inscriptions. A spray of laurel, representing achievement is at the bottom. The ribbon is a field of myrtle green with five white stripes in the center and white edges. The Army Commendation Medal was designed and sculpted by Thomas Hudson Jones of the Institute of Heraldry.

Army Presidential Unit Citation

The Army Presidential Unit Citation *(PUC)* was established on February 26, 1942 as the *"Distinguished Unit Badge"* or the *"Distinguished Unit Citation"* and redesignated as the Presidential Unit Citation in 1966. It is awarded to Army units that display the same degree of heroism in combat as would warrant the Distinguished Service Cross for an individual. Like all Army unit awards, the PUC is worn above the pocket on the right breast of the uniform. The gold-colored frame around the ribbon is worn with the open end of the *"V"* of the laurel leaf pattern pointing upward. The badge may only be worn

Service: Army
Instituted: 1942
Criteria: Awarded to U.S. Army units for extraordinary heroism in action against an armed enemy.
Devices:

permanently by those individuals who were assigned to the unit for the period for which it was cited. Current members of the unit who were not assigned to the unit for the award period are entitled to wear the ribbon but only for the duration of their assignment with the cited unit. Such personnel must remove it from their uniform upon reassignment. Additional awards of the Army Presidential Unit Citation are denoted by bronze and silver oak leaf clusters.

Army Valorous Unit Award

The Army Valorous Unit Award was approved and established by the Army Chief of Staff on January 12, 1966. It is awarded to units of the Armed Forces of the United States for extraordinary heroism in action against an armed enemy of the United States while engaged in conflict with an opposing foreign force on or after August 3, 1963. The Valorous Unit Award requires a lesser degree of gallantry than that required for the Presidential Unit Citation. Nevertheless, the unit must have performed with marked distinction under difficult and hazardous conditions so as to set it apart from the other units participating in the same conflict. The degree of heroism required is the same as that which would warrant award of the Silver Star to an individual. This award will normally be earned by units that have participated in single or successive

Service: Army
Instituted: 1963
Criteria: Awarded to U.S. Army units for outstanding heroism in armed combat against an opposing armed force.
Devices:

actions covering relatively brief time spans but only on rare occasions will a unit larger than a battalion qualify for this award. Additional awards are denoted by bronze and silver oak leaf clusters.

Army Meritorious Unit Commendation

The Army Meritorious Unit Commendation is awarded to units for exceptionally meritorious conduct in performance of outstanding services for at least six continuous months during the period of military operations against an armed enemy occurring on or after January 1, 1944. Service in a combat zone is not required but must be directly related to the combat effort. Units based within the continental U.S. or outside the area of operation are excluded from this award. The unit must display such outstanding devotion and superior performance of exceptionally difficult tasks as to set it apart and above other units with similar missions. The award is usually given to units larger than battalions. The degree of achievement required is the same as that which would warrant award of the Legion of Merit to an individual. It was originally authorized as a wreath emblem that was worn on the lower right sleeve of the Army uniform but

Service: Army and Army Air Force
Instituted: 1944
Criteria: Awarded to U.S. Army units for exceptionally meritorious conduct in the performance of outstanding service.
Devices:

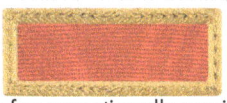

was redeveloped in its present form in 1961. As with other unit citations, it has a gold frame surrounding the ribbon; the open end of the "V" shaped design on the frame points upward and is worn with other unit citations on the right side of the uniform. Additional awards are denoted by bronze and silver oak leaf clusters.

★ Prisoner of War Medal

Service: All Services
Instituted: 1985
Criteria: Awarded to any member of the U.S. Armed Forces taken prisoner during any armed conflict dating from World War I.
Devices:

The Prisoner of War Medal is awarded to any person who was taken prisoner of war and held captive after April 5, 1917. It was authorized by Public Law Number 99-145 in 1985 and may be awarded to any person who was taken prisoner or held captive while engaged in an action against an enemy of the United States, while engaged in military operations involving conflict with an opposing armed force or while serving with friendly forces engaged in armed conflict against an opposing armed force in which the United States is not a belligerent party. The recipient's conduct while a prisoner must have been honorable.

The Prisoner of War Medal is worn after all unit awards *(after personal decorations in the case of the Army)* and before the various Armed Service Good Conduct Medals *(before the Combat Readiness Medal in the case of the Air Force)*.

The Prisoner of War Medal was designed by the Institute of Heraldry. The medal is a circular bronze disc with an American eagle centered and completely surrounded by a ring of barbed wire and bayonet points. The reverse of the medal has a raised inscription, *"AWARDED TO"* with a space for the recipient's name and, *"FOR HONORABLE SERVICE WHILE A PRISONER OF WAR"* set in three lines. Below this is the shield of the United States and the words, *"UNITED STATES OF AMERICA."* The ribbon is black with thin border stripes of white, blue, white and red. Additional awards are denoted by three-sixteenth inch bronze stars.

★ Army Good Conduct Medal

Bronze

Anodized or Gold-Plated

Regulation Ribbon Bar

Enamel Lapel Pin

Medal Reverse

Miniature Medal

Mini Ribbon *(unofficial)*

Army Good Conduct Medal

The ribbon was designed by Arthur E. DuBois, the legendary Director of the Army Institute of Heraldry, and is scarlet with three narrow white stripes on each side. The ribbon is divided by the white stripes so as to form thirteen stripes representing the thirteen original colonies of the United States. During the Revolutionary War, the color scarlet symbolized the mother country and the white stripe symbolized the virgin land separated by force from the mother country.

Unlike other additional award devices, e.g., oak leaf clusters, bronze, silver, or gold clasps with knots *(or loops)* are used to indicate the **total** number of awards of the Army Good Conduct Medal. For instance, two awards of the medal are indicated by two bronze knots, three by three, etc. Six total awards are indicated by one silver knot, seven by two silver knots, etc. Eleven total awards are indicated by one gold knot, twelve by two gold knots, etc. While all regulations since World War II only authorize a clasp to be worn after the second award or higher; it was not unusual to see veterans with a clasp having a single bronze knot on their Army Good Conduct Medal or ribbon; this may have indicated either a single or second award and seems to have been an earlier unofficial practice.

Service	Army
Instituted	1941
Criteria	Exemplary conduct, efficiency and fidelity during three years of active enlisted service with the U.S. Army (1 year during wartime).
Devices	Bronze, Silver, Gold Knotted clasp

Although the Good Conduct Medal was officially instituted by executive order in 1941, it really goes back to the American Revolution. When General George Washington established the Badge of Military Merit in 1782 he also created an award called the Honorary Badge of Distinction. This was the first good conduct award since it was to be conferred on veteran noncommissioned officers and soldiers of the Army who served more than three years with bravery, fidelity and good conduct. However, just as the Badge of Military Merit disappeared after the Revolution so did the Honorary Badge of Distinction.

Army Reserve Components Achievement Medal

Authorized by the Secretary of the Army on March 3, 1971 and amended by Dept. of the Army General Order 4, 1974, this medal is awarded to any person in the rank of Colonel or below for exemplary behavior, efficiency and fidelity while serving as a member of the Army National Guard (ARNG), a United States Army Reserve troop program unit (TPU) or as an individual augmentee.

The medal is 1-$\frac{1}{4}$ inches in diameter. In the center is a flaming torch symbolizing the vigilance of the Guard and the Reserve and their readiness to come to the Nation's aid. Two crossed swords in front of and behind the torch represent the history of the Guard and Reserve forged in combat. Left and right of the torch are five pointed stars and the entire design is surrounded by a laurel wreath symbolizing accomplishment. Around these symbols is a twelve pointed star superimposed over a smaller twelve-pointed star indicating the Guard and Reserve's ability to travel where needed in the United States or the world. In between the points of the larger star are laurel leaves and a berry representing achievement.

On the reverse side of the medal in the upper center is a miniature breast plate taken from the Army seal. Above this, the outside edge of the medal is inscribed either, "UNITED STATES ARMY RESERVE" or "ARMY NATIONAL GUARD." Along the bottom edge of the medal are the words, "FOR ACHIEVEMENT."

Service: Army

Instituted: 1971

Criteria: Exemplary conduct, efficiency and fidelity during 3 years of service with the U.S. Army Reserve or National Guard.

Devices:

The ribbon has a wide center stripe of red flanked by narrow stripes of white and blue, reflecting our national colors and patriotism. The outside gold stripes are symbolic of merit. Additional awards are denoted by bronze and silver oak leaf clusters.

⭐ American Defense Service Medal

Service: All Services
Instituted: 1941
Dates: 1939-41
Criteria: Army: 12 months of active duty service during the above period; Naval Services: Any active duty service.
Devices:

Navy: FLEET
Navy: BASE
Army: FOREIGN SERVICE
Coast Guard: SEA

Bars: "Foreign Service", "Base", "Fleet", "Sea"

⭐ American Campaign Medal

Service: All Services
Instituted: 1942
Dates: 1941-46
Criteria: Service outside the U.S. in the American theater for 30 days, or within the continental U.S. for one year.
Devices:

World War II and Korean War Medals are shown because there were veterans of both wars who served in Vietnam and therefore would have their previous campaign medals along with their Vietnam service medals.

⭐ Asia-Pacific Campaign Medal

Service: All Services
Instituted: 1942
Dates: 1941-46
Criteria: Service in the Asiatic-Pacific theater for 30 days or receipt of any combat decoration.
Devices:

⭐ European-African-Middle Eastern Campaign Medal

Service: All Services
Instituted: 1942
Dates: 1941-45
Criteria: Service in the European-African-Middle Eastern theater for 30 days or receipt of any combat decoration.
Devices:

Bronze Arrowhead
Silver Campaign Star
Bronze Campaign Star

World War II Victory Medal

Authorized by an Act of Congress on July 6, 1945 and awarded to all members of the Armed Forces who served at least one day of honorable, active federal service between December 7, 1941 and December 31, 1946, inclusive.

The front of the medal depicts the Liberty figure resting her right foot on a war god's helmet with the hilt of a broken sword in her right hand and the broken blade in her left hand. The reverse contains the words, *"FREEDOM FROM FEAR AND WANT, FREEDOM OF SPEECH AND RELIGION,* and *UNITED STATES OF AMERICA 1941-1945."* The red center stripe of the ribbon is symbolic of Mars, the God of War, representing both courage and fortitude. The twin rainbow stripes, suggested by the World War I Victory Medal, allude to the peace following a storm. A narrow white stripe separates the center red stripe from each rainbow pattern on both sides of the ribbon. The World War II Victory Medal provides deserving recognition to all of America's veterans who served during World War II.

No attachments are authorized although some veterans received the medal with an affixed bronze star which, according to rumors at the time, was to distinguish those who served in combat from those who did not. However, no official documentation has ever been found to support this supposition. Although eligible for its award, many World War II veterans never actually received the medal since many were discharged prior to the medal's being struck in late 1946.

Service: All Services
Instituted: 1945
Dates: 1941-46
Criteria: Awarded for service in the U.S. Armed Forces during the above period.
Devices: None

Army of Occupation Medal

Service: Army/Air Force
Instituted: 1946
Dates: 1945-55 (Berlin: 1945-90)
Criteria: 30 consecutive days of service in occupied territories of former enemies during above period.
Devices:

Bars:
Germany Clasp   Japan Clasp

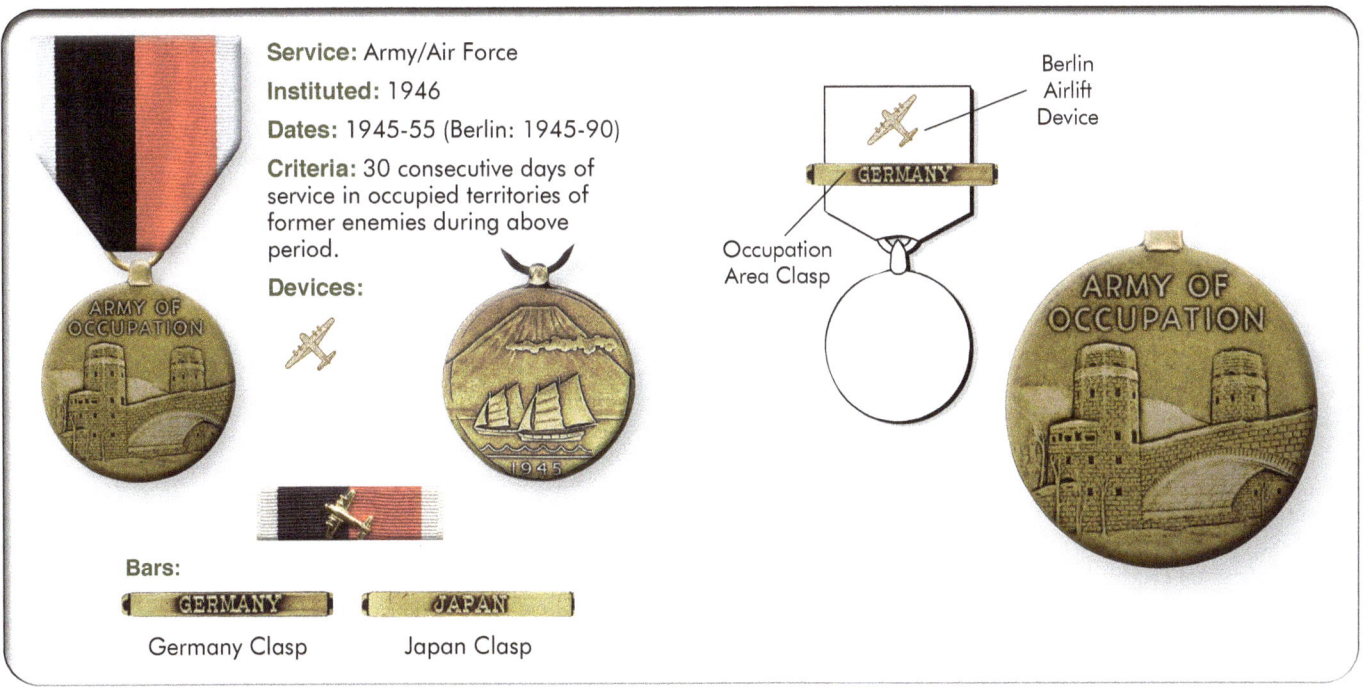

Berlin Airlift Device
Occupation Area Clasp

Medal for Humane Action

Service: All Services
Instituted: 1949
Dates: 1948-49
Criteria: 120 consecutive days of service participating in the Berlin Airlift or in support thereof. Was also awarded posthumously.
Devices: None
Notes: This medal was only awarded for Berlin Airlift service and is not to be confused with the Humanitarian Service Medal (established in 1977).

National Defense Service Medal

Initially authorized by executive order on April 22, 1953. It is awarded to members of the U.S. Armed Forces for any honorable active federal service during the Korean War *(June 27, 1950 - July 27, 1954)*, Vietnam War *(January 1, 1961- August 14, 1974)*, Desert Shield/Desert Storm *(August 2, 1990 - November 30, 1995)* and/or Operations Iraqi Freedom and Enduring Freedom *(Afghanistan) (September 11, 2001 to a date TBD)*. President Bush issued an Executive Order 12776 on October 8, 1991 authorizing award of the medal to all members of the Reserve forces whether or not on active duty during the designated period of the Gulf War.

The latest award of the medal was promulgated in a memo, dated April 2, 2002, from the Office of the Deputy Secretary of Defense, Mr. Paul Wolfowitz who authorized the award to all U.S. Service Members on duty on or after September 11, 2001 to 31 Dec. 2022. Today, there are probably more people authorized this medal than any other award in U.S. history. Circumstances not qualifying as active duty for the purpose of this medal include: (1) Members of the Guard and Reserve on short tours of active duty to fulfill training obligations; (2) Service members on active duty to serve on boards, courts, commissions, and like organizations; (3) Service members on active duty for the sole purpose of undergoing a physical examination; and (4) Service members on active duty for purposes other than extended active duty. Reserve personnel who have received the Armed Forces Expeditionary Medal or the Vietnam Service Medal are eligible for this medal.

The National Defense Service Medal is also authorized to those individuals serving as cadets or midshipmen at the Air Force, Army or Naval Academies. The front of the medal shows the American bald eagle with inverted wings standing on a

Service: All Services
Instituted: 1953
Dates: 1950-54, 1961-74, 1990-95, 2001 - TBD
Criteria: Any honorable active duty service during any of the above periods.
Devices:
Notes: Reinstituted in 1966, 1991 and 2001 for Vietnam, Southwest Asia (Gulf War) and Iraq/Afghanistan actions respectively.

sword and palm branch and contains the words, *"NATIONAL DEFENSE"*; the reverse has the United States shield amidst an oak leaf and laurel spray. Symbolically, the eagle is the national emblem of the United States, the sword represents the Armed Forces and the palm is symbolic of victory. The reverse contains the shield from the great seal of the United States flanked by a wreath of laurel and oak representing achievement and strength. The ribbon has a broad center stripe of yellow representing high ideals. The red, white and blue stripes represent the national flag. Red for hardiness and valor, white for purity of purpose and blue for perseverance and justice. No more than one medal is awarded to a single individual but a three-sixteenth inch diameter. bronze star denotes an additional award of the medal.

Korean Service Medal

Authorized by executive order on November 8, 1950 and awarded for service between June 27, 1950 and July 27, 1954 in the Korean theater of operations. Members of the U.S. Armed Forces must have participated in combat or served with a combat or service unit in the Korean Theater for 30 consecutive or 60 nonconsecutive days during the designated period. Personnel who served with a unit or headquarters stationed outside the theater but in direct support of Korean military operations are also entitled to this medal. The combat zone designated for qualification for the medal encompassed both North and South Korea, Korean waters and the airspace over these areas. The first campaign began when North Korea first invaded South Korea and the last campaign ended when the Korean Armistice cease-fire became effective. The period of Korean service was extended by one year from the cease fire by the Secretary of Defense; individuals could qualify for the medal during this period if stationed in Korea but would not receive any campaign credit. An award of this medal qualifies personnel for award of the United Nations *(Korean)* Service Medal and the Republic of Korea War Service Medal *(approved 1999)*.

A Korean gateway is depicted on the front of the medal along with the inscription, *"KOREAN SERVICE"* and on the reverse are the "Taeguk" symbol from the Korean flag that represents unity and the inscription, *"UNITED STATES OF AMERICA."* A spray of oak and laurel line the bottom edge. The suspension ribbon and ribbon bar are both blue and white representing the United Nations. Bronze and silver stars are affixed to the suspension drape and ribbon bar to indicate participation in any of the 10 designated campaigns in the Korean War. Army personnel who participated in an amphibious assault landing are entitled to wear the arrowhead attachment.

Service: All Services
Instituted: 1950
Dates: 1950-54
Criteria: Participation in military operations within the Korean area during the above period.
Devices:

Antarctica Service Medal

Authorized on July 7, 1960 and awarded to any member of the Armed Forces who, from January 2, 1946, as a member of a U.S. Antarctic expedition, participates in, or performs services in direct support of scientific or exploratory operations on the Antarctic Continent. Qualifying service includes personnel who participate in flights or naval operations supporting operations in Antarctica. The medal may also be awarded to any U.S. citizen who participates in Antarctic expeditions under the same conditions as Service personnel.

The front of the medal depicts a figure appropriately clothed in cold weather gear with his hood thrown back, arms extended and legs spread, symbolizing stability, determination, courage and devotion. The reverse depicts a map of the Antarctic continent in polar projection across which are three centered lines containing the inscription, *"COURAGE SACRIFICE DEVOTION."*

A clasp containing the raised inscription, *"WINTERED OVER"* is worn on the medal and a disc of the same metal, containing the outline of the Antarctic Continent is worn on the ribbon bar if the individual remains on the continent during the winter months. For the first stay, the disc and bar are made of bronze, for the second stay, they are gold-colored and for the third and all subsequent winter tours, the devices are silver.

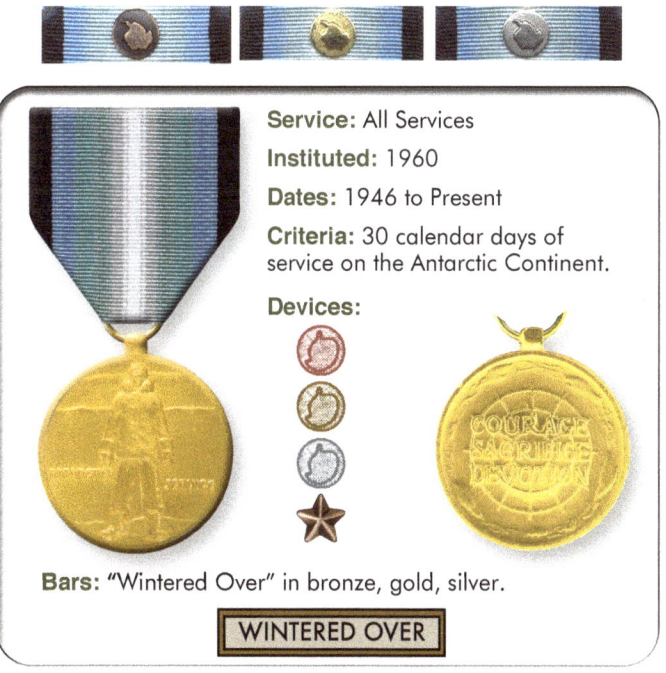

Service: All Services
Instituted: 1960
Dates: 1946 to Present
Criteria: 30 calendar days of service on the Antarctic Continent.
Devices:

Bars: "Wintered Over" in bronze, gold, silver.

Armed Forces Expeditionary Medal

President John F. Kennedy characterized the post World War II period as *"a twilight that is neither peace nor war."* During the period commonly referred to as the Cold War, the Armed Services agreed to one medal to recognize major actions not otherwise covered by a specific campaign medal.

The Armed Forces Expeditionary Medal was authorized on December 4, 1961 to any member of the United States Armed Forces for U.S. military operations, U.S. operations in direct support of the United Nations and U.S. operations of assistance to friendly foreign nations after July 1, 1958. Operations that qualify for this medal are authorized in specific orders. Participating personnel must have served at least 30 consecutive (60 nonconsecutive) days in the qualifying operation or less if the operation was less than 30 days in length. The medal may also be authorized for individuals who do not meet the basic criteria but who do merit special recognition for their service in the designated operation.

The first qualifying operation was Operation Blue Bat, a peacekeeping mission in Lebanon from July 1 to November 1, 1958. This medal was initially awarded for Vietnam service between July 1, 1958 and July 3, 1965; an individual awarded the medal for this period of Vietnam service may elect to keep the award or request the Vietnam Service Medal in its place. However, both awards may not be retained for the same period of Vietnam service. Many personnel received this medal for continuing service in Cambodia after the Vietnam cease-fire. The medal was also authorized for those serving in the Persian Gulf area who previously would have qualified for the Southwest Asia Service Medal and the National Defense Service Medal whose qualification periods for that area terminated on November 30, 1995. Individuals who qualify for both the Southwest Asia Service Medal and the Armed Forces Expeditionary Medal must elect to receive the Expeditionary medal.

The front of the medal depicts an American eagle with wings raised, perched on a sword. Behind this is a compass rose with rays coming from the angles of the compass points. The words *"ARMED FORCES EXPEDITIONARY SERVICE"* encircle the design. The reverse of the medal depicts the Presidential shield with branches of laurel below and the inscription, *"UNITED STATES OF AMERICA."* The American national colors are located at the center position or honor point of the ribbon. The light blue sections on either side suggest water and overseas service, while various colors representing areas of the world where American troops may be called upon to serve run outward to the edge.

Service: All Services
Instituted: 1961
Dates: 1958 to Present
Criteria: Participation in military operations not covered by specific war medal.
Devices:

Notes: Authorized for service in Vietnam until establishment of Vietnam Service Medal.

Army
Bronze Arrowhead
Silver Campaign Star
Bronze Campaign Stars

The qualifying campaigns:

- Lebanon, Jul. 1, 1958 - Nov. 1, 1958
- Taiwan Straits, Aug. 23, 1958 - Jan. 1, 1959
- Quemoy & Matsu Islands, Aug. 23, 1958 - Jun. 1, 1963
- Vietnam, Jul. 1, 1958 - Jul. 3, 1965
- Congo, Jul. 14, 1960 - Sep. 1, 1962
- Laos, Apr. 19, 1961 - Oct. 7, 1962
- Berlin, Aug. 14, 1961 - Jun. 1, 1963
- Cuba, Oct. 24, 1962 - Jun. 1, 1963
- Congo, Nov. 23-27, 1964
- Dominican Republic, Apr. 23, 1965 - Sep. 21, 1966
- Korea, Oct. 1, 1966 - Jun. 30, 1974
- Cambodia, Mar. 29, 1973 - Aug. 15, 1973
- Thailand, Mar. 29, 1973 - Aug. 15, 1973 (Only those in direct support of Cambodia)
- Operation Eagle Pull - Cambodia, Apr. 11-13, 1975 (Includes evacuation)
- Operation Frequent Wind - Vietnam, Apr. 29-30, 1975
- Mayaquez Operation, May 15, 1975
- El Salvador, Jan. 1, 1981 - Feb. 1, 1992
- Lebanon, Jun. 1, 1983 - Dec. 1, 1987
- Operation Urgent Fury - Grenada, Oct. 23, 1983 - Nov. 21, 1983
- Eldorado Canyon - Libya, Apr. 12-17, 1986
- ★ Operation Earnest Will - Persian Gulf, Jul. 24, 1987 - Aug. 1, 1990 (Only those participating in, or in direct support)
- ★ Operation Just Cause - Panama, Dec. 20, 1989 - Jan. 31, 1990 (USS Vreeland & other SVS-designated aircrew mbrs. outside the Conus in direct support)
- ★ United Shield - Somalia, Dec. 5, 1992 - Mar. 31, 1995
- ★ Operation Restore Hope - Somalia, Dec. 5, 1992 - Mar. 31, 1995
- ★ Operation Uphold Democracy - Haiti, Sept. 1994 - Mar. 31, 1995
- ★ Operation Joint Endeavor - Bosnia, Croatia, the Adriatic Sea & Airspace, Nov. 20, 1995 - Dec. 19, 1996
- ★ Operation Vigilant Sentinel - Iraq, Saudi Arabia, Kuwait, & Persian Gulf, Dec. 1, 1995 - Sep. 1, 1997
- ★ Operation Southern Watch - Iraq, Saudi Arabia, Kuwait, Persian Gulf, Bahrain, Qatar, UAE, Oman, Gulf of Oman W of 62° E Long., Yemen, Egypt, & Jordan
- ★ Operation Maritime Intercept - Iraq, Saudi Arabia, Kuwait, Red Sea, Persian Gulf, Gulf of Oman W of 62° E Long., Bahrain, Qatar, UAE, Oman, Yemen, Egypt & Jordan Dec. 1, 1995 - Open
- ★ Operation Joint Guard - Bosnia, Herzegovina, Croatia, Adriatic Sea & Airspace, Dec. 20, 1996 - Jun. 20, 2008
- ★ Operation Northern Watch - Iraq, Saudi Arabia, Kuwait, Persian Gulf of W of 56° E Long., and Incirlik AB, Turkey (Only pers. TDY to ONW), Jan. 1, 1997 - 18 March 2003
- ★ Operation Joint Forge - Bosnia-Herzegovina, Croatia, Adriatic Sea & Airspace, Jun. 21, 1998 - Open
- ★ Operation Desert Thunder - Iraq, Saudi Arabia, Kuwait, Bahrain, Qatar, UAE, Omar, Yemen, Egypt, Jordan, Persian Gulf, Gulf of Oman, Red Sea support, Nov. 11, 1998 - Dec. 22, 1998
- Operation Desert Fox - Iraq, Saudi Arabia, Kuwait, Bahrain, Qatar, UAE, Oman, Yemen, Egypt, Jordan, Persian Gulf, Gulf of Oman, USN Red Sea support, 16 Dec. - 22 Dec. 1998
- ★ Operation Desert Spring, Haiti, Southwest Asia, 31 Dec. 1998-18 Mar. 2003
- ★ Operation Secure Tomorrow, 29 Feb. 2004 - 15 Jun. 2004

Vietnam Service Medal

Regulation Ribbon Bar

Enamel Lapel Pin

Bronze Anodized or Gold-Plated Medal Reverse

Miniature Medals

Mini Ribbon *(unofficial)*

Hat Pin *(unofficial)*

Authorized by executive order on July 8, 1965 for U.S. military personnel serving in the Vietnam Theater of Operations after July 3, 1965 through March 28, 1973. Personnel must have served in Vietnam on temporary duty for at least 30 consecutive/60 nonconsecutive days or have served in combat with a unit directly supporting a military operation in Southeast Asia. Military personnel serving in Laos, Cambodia or Thailand in direct support of operations in Vietnam are also eligible for this award. The Armed Forces Expeditionary Medal was awarded for earlier service in Vietnam from July 1, 1958 to July 3, 1965, inclusive; personnel receiving that award may be awarded the Vietnam Service Medal but are not authorized both awards for Vietnam service.

The front of the medal depicts an oriental dragon behind a grove of bamboo trees; below the base of the trees is the inscription, *"REPUBLIC OF VIETNAM SERVICE."* The reverse of the medal depicts a crossbow with a torch through the center and contains the inscription, *"UNITED STATES OF AMERICA"* along the bottom edge. The colors of the suspension drape and ribbon suggest the flag of the Republic of Vietnam *(the red stripes represent the three ancient Vietnamese empires of Tonkin, Annam, and Cochin China)* and the green represents the Vietnamese jungle. Bronze and silver stars are authorized to signify participation in any of the 17 designated campaigns during the inclusive period.

Service	All Services
Instituted	1965
Dates	1965-73
Criteria	Service in Vietnam, Laos, Cambodia or Thailand during the above period.
Devices	Bronze, Silver star, Arrowhead

Campaigns Designated by the Army for the Vietnam Service Medal

1. **Vietnam (VN) Advisory -** Mar 15, 1962 to Mar 7, 1965
2. **VN Defense -** Mar 8, 1965 to Dec 24, 1965
3. **VN Counteroffensive -** Dec 25, 1965 to Jun 30, 1966
4. **VN Counteroffensive Phase II -** July 1, 1966 to May 31, 1967
5. **VN Counteroffensive Phase III -** Jun 1, 1967 to Jan 29, 1968
6. **TET Counteroffensive -** Jan 30, 1968 to Apr 1, 1968
7. **VN Counteroffensive Phase IV -** Apr 2, 1968 to Jun 30, 1968
8. **VN Counteroffensive Phase V -** July 1, 1968 to Nov 1, 1968
9. **VN Counteroffensive Phase VI -** Nov 2, 1968 to Feb 22, 1969
10. **TET69 Counteroffensive -** Feb 23, 1969 to Jun 8, 1969
11. **Vietnam Summer -** Fall 1969 - Jun 9, 1969 to Oct 31, 1969
12. **Vietnam Winter-** Spring 1970 - Nov 1, 1969 to Apr 30, 1970
13. **Sanctuary Counteroffensive -** May 1, 1970 to Jun 30, 1970
14. **VN Counteroffensive Campaign Phase VII -** Jul 1, 1970 to Jun 30, 1971
15. **Consolidation I -** Jul 1, 1971 to Nov 30, 1971
16. **Consolidation II -** Dec 1, 1971 to Mar 29, 1972
17. **Vietnam Cease-fire -** Mar 30, 1972 to Jan 28, 1973

⭐ Korea Defense Service Medal

For the defense of the Republic of Korea. The Korea Defense Service Medal is worn after the Global War on Terrorism Service Medal and before the Armed Forces Service Medal.

The Korea Defense Service Medal was provided for in the Fiscal Year 2003 National Defense Authorization Act. The medal is awarded to members of the Armed Forces who served in the Republic of Korea or waters adjacent thereto for a qualifying period of time between July 28, 1954 and a date to be determined.

The Korea Defense Service Medal was designed by the Institute of Heraldry. The medal is a circular bronze disc bearing a Korean circle dragon within an encircling scroll inscribed, *"KOREA DEFENSE SERVICE"* with, in base, two sprigs, laurel to dexter side, bamboo to sinister. Symbolism: The four-clawed dragon is a traditional symbol of Korea and represents intelligence and strength of purpose. The sprig of laurel denotes honorable endeavor and victory, the bamboo refers to the land of Korea. The medal's reverse displays a representation of the land mass of Korea surmounted by two swords points up saltirewise within a circlet with five points.

Symbolism: The swords placed saltirewise over a map of Korea signify defense of freedom in that country and the readiness to engage in combat to that end. The circlet enclosing the device recalls the forms of five-petal symbols common in Korean armory.

Service: All Services
Instituted: 2003
Dates: 1954-TBD
Criteria: For service in the Republic of Korea, or the waters adjacent thereto, for a qualifying period of time between 28 July, 1954 and a date to be determined.
Devices: None

New design without word "Medal"

Earlier design with the word "Medal"

The ribbon is dark green representing the land of Korea, blue indicates overseas service and commitment to achieving peace. Gold denotes excellence, white symbolizes idealism and integrity. Light blue with a thin white stripe in the center and narrow white stripes at the edges.

★ Armed Forces Reserve Medal

Bronze

Anodized or Gold-Plated

Regulation Ribbon Bar

Enamel Lapel Pin

Army Medal Reverse

Mini Ribbon *(unofficial)*

Enamel Hat Pin *(unofficial)*

Miniature Medals

Authorized in 1950 for 10 years of honorable and satisfactory service within a 12 year period as a member of one or more of the Reserve Components of the Armed Forces of the United States.

An executive order of Aug. 8, 1996 authorized the award of a bronze letter "M" mobilization device to U.S. reserve component members who were called to active-duty service in support of designated operations on or after August 1, 1990 *(the M device was not authorized for any operations prior to August 1, 1990 although it had been previously proposed)*. Units called up in support of Operations Desert Storm/Desert Shield were the first units to be authorized the "M" device. If an "M" is authorized, the medal is awarded even though service might be less than 10 years. Previous to this change, only bronze hourglasses were awarded at each successive 10 year point *(first hourglass at the 20 year point)*.

The front of the medal depicts a flaming torch placed vertically between a crossed bugle and powder horn; thirteen stars and thirteen rays surround the design. The front of the

Service	All Services
Instituted	1950
Criteria	10 years of honorable service in any reserve component of the United States Armed Forces Reserve or award of "M" device.
Devices	Bronze, Silver and Gold Hourglass, Bronze Letter "M", Bronze Numeral

medal is the same for all services; only the reverse design is different *(see designs below)*. Bronze numerals beginning with *"2"* are worn to the right of the bronze *"M"* on the ribbon bar and on the medal, indicating the total number of times the individual was mobilized. Bronze, silver and gold hourglasses are awarded for 10, 20 and 30 years service, respectively.

The different services medal reverses are shown here:

Air Force has the Air force Seal in the Center.

Navy has a sailing ship with an anchor on its front with an eagle with wings spread superimposed upon it.

Marine Corps has the USMC emblem, eagle, globe and anchor.

Coast Guard has the Coast Guard emblem, crossed anchor with the Coast Guard shield in the center.

National Guard has the National Guard insignia on the reverse, an eagle with crossed fasces in its center.

Award of Foreign Military Decorations

Authorized foreign decorations for wear by United States Armed Forces are military decorations *(as opposed to service medals)* which have been approved for wear by the Department of Defense but whose awarding authority is a foreign government. French British, Italian and other Allies decorations were presented to U.S. service members extensively during World War I and World War II. In World War I and II the French and Belgium Croix de Guerre were the most commonly awarded decorations to United States service members of all ranks.

Republic of Vietnam military awards *(South Vietnam decorations)* were first awarded to United States service members beginning around 1964. The Vietnamese Gallantry Cross and the Vietnamese Civil Actions Medal were awarded to many U.S. servicemen for heroism and meritorious service.

Foreign campaign *(service)* medals and unit awards have also been awarded U.S. military personnel. Those that were commonly awarded to U.S. military personnel are covered in the following pages.

While each service has its own order of precedence, these general rules typically apply to all services when wearing foreign awards:

- U.S. military personal decorations
- U.S. military unit awards
- U.S. non-military personal decorations (in order of receipt; if from the same service.
- U.S. non-military unit awards
- U.S. military campaign and service medals
- U.S. military service and training awards (ribbon-only awards)
- U.S. Merchant Marine awards and non-military service awards
- Foreign military personal decorations
- Foreign military unit awards
- International decorations & service medals (United Nations, NATO, etc.)
- Foreign military service awards
- Marksmanship awards (Air Force, Navy & Coast Guard)
- State awards of the National Guard (Army & Air Force only)

The Military Ribbons of the Republic of Vietnam

Starting in the upper left-hand corner are military Decorations and Service Medals of the Republic of Vietnam. The awards are listed in the column to the right.

Not shown: Medal for Campaigns Outside the Frontier and the Air Force Northern Expeditionary Medal

National Order of Vietnam, Commander (3rd class)
National Order of Vietnam, Knight or fifth class
Military Merit Medal
Army Distinguished Service Order 1st class
Army Distinguished Service Order 2d class
Air Force Distinguished Service Order
Navy Distinguished Service Order
Army Meritorious Service Medal
Air Force Meritorious Service Medal
Navy Meritorious Service Medal
Gallantry Cross with bronze star
Air Force Gallantry Cross
Navy Gallantry Cross
Special Service Medal
Hazardous Service Medal
Lifesaving Medal
Loyalty Medal
Wound Medal
Armed Honor Medal first class
Armed Honor Medal second class
Leadership Medal
Staff service Medal first class
Staff service Medal second class
Technical Service Medal first class
Technical Service Medal second class
Training Service Medal first & second class
Civic Actions Medal first class
Civic Action Medal second class
Good Conduct Medal
Campaign Medal
Military Service Medal
Air Service Medal
Navy Service Medal, Unity Medal, Medal of Sacrifice

South Vietnamese Medals with Certificates

Gallantry Cross

Armed Forces Honor Medal First Class

Ethnic Development Medal First Class Civilian Award

Psychological Warfare Medal First Class and Second Class

South Vietnamese Decorations Generally Awarded

Republic of Vietnam Gallantry Cross

Country: Republic of Vietnam
Instituted: 1950
Criteria: Deeds of valor and acts of courage/heroism while fighting the enemy.
Devices:
- Army level award
- Corps level award
- Division level award
- Regt. level award

Republic of Vietnam Armed Forces Honor Medal

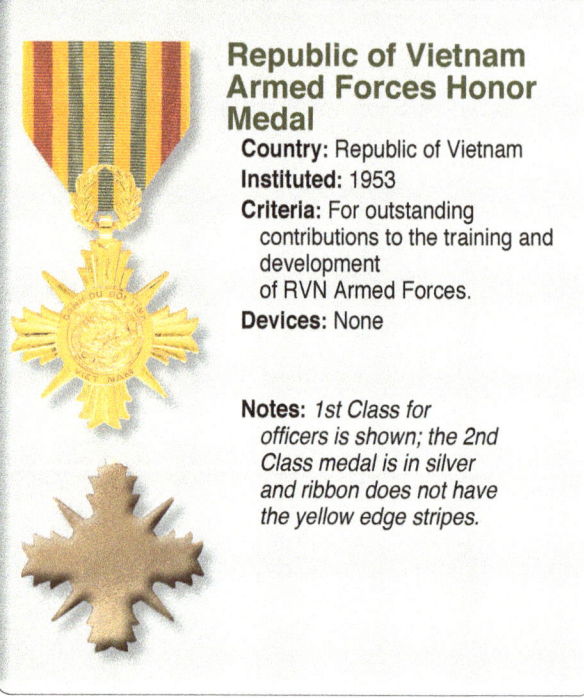

Country: Republic of Vietnam
Instituted: 1953
Criteria: For outstanding contributions to the training and development of RVN Armed Forces.
Devices: None

Notes: 1st Class for officers is shown; the 2nd Class medal is in silver and ribbon does not have the yellow edge stripes.

Republic of Vietnam Staff Service Medal

Country: Republic of Vietnam
Instituted: 1964
Criteria: Awarded for staff service to the Armed Forces evidencing outstanding initiative and devotion to duty.

Notes: Occasionally called Staff Service Honor Medal. First class has green edge, 2d class for enlisted has blue ribbon edge.

First Class — Second Class

Republic of Vietnam Technical Service Medal

Country: Republic of Vietnam
Instituted: 1964
Criteria: Awarded to military servicemen and civilians working as military technicians who have shown outstanding professional capacity, initiative, and devotion to duty.

Notes: Second Class medal ribbon awarded to NCOs and enlisted men does not have 2 center red stripes. Occasionally called Technical Services Honor Medal.

First Class

Republic of Vietnam Training Medal

Country: Republic of Vietnam
Instituted: 1964
Criteria: Awarded to instructors and cadres at military schools and training centers and civilians and foreigners who contribute significantly to training.

Notes: First Class medal is awarded to officers and is occasionally referred to as the Training Service Honor Medal. Second Class medal ribbon awarded to NCOs and enlisted men does not have 2 center pink stripes.

Republic of Vietnam Civil Actions Medal

Country: Republic of Vietnam
Instituted: 1964
Criteria: For outstanding achievements in the field of civic actions.
Devices: None

Notes: 1st Class for officers is shown; the 2nd Class ribbon has no center red stripes. Also awarded as a unit award. Sometimes called Civic Actions Honor Medal.

40 Medals, Badges and Insignia U.S. Army Vietnam

Commonly Awarded Foreign Unit Awards

Philippine Republic Presidential Unit Citation

Service: All Services
Instituted: 1948
Criteria: Awarded to units of the U.S. Armed Forces for service in the war against Japan and/or for 1970 and 1972 disaster relief.
Devices: None

The Philippine Republic Presidential Unit Citation was awarded to U.S. Armed Forces personnel for services resulting in the liberation of the Philippines during World War II. The award was made in the name of the President of the Republic of the Philippines. It was also awarded to U.S. Forces who participated in disaster relief operations in 1970 and 1972. The ribbon has three equal stripes of blue, white and red enclosed in a rectangular gold frame with laurel leaves identical to U.S. unit awards.

Korean Republic Presidential Unit Citation

Service: All Services
Instituted: 1951
Criteria: Awarded to certain units of the U.S. Armed Forces for services rendered during the Korean War.
Devices: None

Awarded by the Republic of Korea for service in a unit cited in the name of the President of the Republic of Korea for outstanding performance in action. The Republic of Korea Presidential Unit Citation was awarded to units of the United Nations Command for service in Korea during the Korean Conflict from 1950 to 1954. The ribbon is white bordered with a wide green stripe and thin stripes of white, red, white, red, white and green. In the center is an ancient oriental symbol called a Taeguk *(the top half is red and the bottom half is blue)*. The ribbon is enclosed in a rectangular gold frame with laurel leaves identical to U.S. unit awards. No devices are authorized.

Republic of Vietnam Presidential Unit Citation

Service: Army/Navy/Marine Corps/Coast Guard
Instituted: 1954
Criteria: Awarded to certain units of the U.S. Armed Forces for humanitarian service in the evacuation of civilians from North and Central Vietnam.
Devices: None

Awarded by the Republic of Vietnam for service in a unit cited in the name of the President of the Republic of Vietnam for outstanding performance in action. The Republic of Vietnam Presidential Unit Citation referred to as the "Friendship Ribbon" and was awarded to members of the United States Military Assistance Advisory Group in Indochina for services rendered during August and September 1954. The ribbon is yellow with three narrow red stripes in the center. The ribbon is enclosed in a rectangular gold frame with laurel leaves identical to U.S. unit awards. No devices are authorized.

Republic of Vietnam Gallantry Cross Unit Citation

Service: All Services
Instituted: 1966
Criteria: Awarded to certain units of the U.S. Armed Forces for valorous combat achievement during the Vietnam War, 1 March 1961 to 28 March 1974.
Devices:

The Republic of Vietnam Gallantry Cross Unit Citation was established on August 15, 1950 and awarded by the Republic of Vietnam to units of the U.S. Armed Forces in recognition of valorous achievement in combat during the Vietnam War. The Republic of Vietnam Gallantry Cross Unit Citation ribbon is red with a very wide yellow center stripe which has eight very thin double red stripes. The ribbon bar is enclosed in a gold frame with laurel leaves identical to U.S. unit awards.

Republic of Vietnam Civil Actions Unit Citation

Service: All Services
Instituted: 1966
Criteria: Awarded to certain units of the U.S. Armed Forces for meritorious service during the Vietnam War, 1 March 1961 to 28 March 1974.
Devices:

Awarded by the Republic of Vietnam to units in recognition of meritorious civil action service. The Republic of Vietnam Civil Actions Unit Citation was widely bestowed on American forces in Vietnam and recognizes outstanding achievements made by units in the field of civil affairs. The Republic of Vietnam Civil Actions Unit Citation ribbon is dark green with a very thin double red center stripe narrow red stripes near the edges. The ribbon is enclosed in a rectangular one-sixteenth inch gold frame with laurel leaves identical to U.S. unit awards and is awarded with a bronze laurel leaf palm attachment.

World War II Philippine Military Medals

Philippine Defense Medal
Country: Republic of the Philippines
Instituted: 1945 (Army: 1948)
Criteria: Service in defense of the Philippines between 8 December 1941 and 15 June 1942.
Devices:

Philippine Liberation Medal
Country: Republic of the Philippines
Instituted: 1945 (Army: 1948)
Criteria: Service in the liberation of the Philippines between 17 October 1944 and 3 September 1945.
Devices:

The Philippine Defense Medal was authorized to any WW II veteran of either the Philippine military or an allied armed force, to recognize the initial resistance against Japanese invasion between 8 December 1941 and 15 June 1942. The award was first created in December 1944, and was issued as the Philippine Defense Ribbon. A full-sized medal was authorized and added in July, 1945.

The Philippine Liberation Medal was established by the Commonwealth Army of the Philippines on 20 December 1944, and first issued as a Ribbon. The medal was presented to Philippine Commonwealth and allied forces, who participated in the liberation of the Philippine Islands between t 17 October 1944, and 2 September 1945. A full-sized medal was authorized and added on 22 July 1945 and authorized by the United States in 1948.

The Philippine Independence Medal was established by the Philippine Army 3 July 1946 as the Philippine Independence Ribbon. The medal was added in 1968. The medal's criteria effectively awarded the medal to anyone who had participated in both the

Philippine Independence Medal
Country: Republic of the Philippines
Instituted: 1946 (Army: 1948)
Criteria: Receipt of both the Philippine Defense and Liberation Medals/Ribbons. Originally presented to those present for duty in the Philippines on 4 July 1946.
Devices: None

initial resistance against Japanese invasion and also in the campaigns to liberate the Philippines from Japanese occupation in 1945. The medal was also authorized for award to the United States personnel in the Philippines up to 1948.

United Nations Medal

United Nations Service Medal (Korea)
Service: All Services
Instituted: 1951
Criteria: Service on behalf of the United Nations in Korea between 27 June 1950 and 27 July 1954.
Devices: None
Notes: Above date denotes when award was authorized for wear by U.S. military personnel.

42 Medals, Badges and Insignia U.S. Army Vietnam

⭐ Republic of Vietnam Campaign Medal

The Republic of Vietnam Campaign Medal was established by the Government of the Republic of Vietnam on May 12, 1964 and authorized for award to members of the United States Armed Forces by the Department of Defense on June 20, 1966. To qualify for award, personnel must meet one of the following requirements:

(1) Have served in the Republic of Vietnam for 6 months during the period from March 1, 1961 to March 28, 1973.
(2) Have served outside the geographical limits of the Republic of Vietnam and contributed direct combat support to the Republic of Vietnam and Armed Forces for six months. Such individuals must meet the criteria established for the Armed Forces Expeditionary Medal *(Vietnam)* or the Vietnam Service Medal, during the period of service required to qualify for the Republic of Vietnam Campaign Medal.
(3) Have served for less than six months and have been wounded by hostile forces, captured by hostile forces, but later escaped, was rescued or released or killed in action.

Special eligibility rules were established for personnel assigned in the Republic of Vietnam on January 28, 1973. To be eligible for the medal, an individual must have served a minimum of 60 days in the Republic of Vietnam as of that date or have completed a minimum of 60 days service in the Republic of Vietnam during the period from January 28, 1973 to March 28, 1973, inclusive.

The Republic of Vietnam Campaign Medal is a white

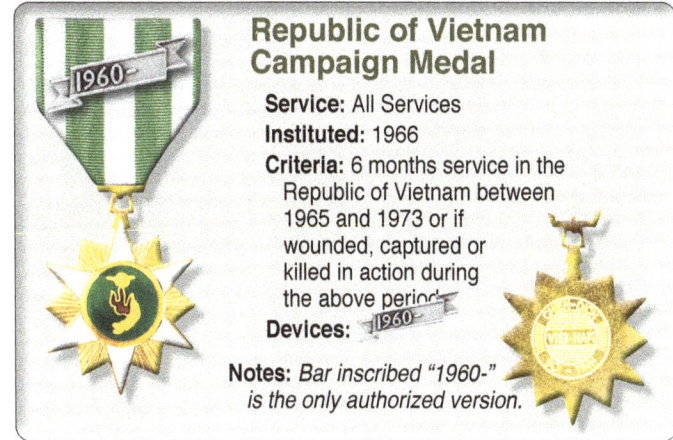

Republic of Vietnam Campaign Medal
Service: All Services
Instituted: 1966
Criteria: 6 months service in the Republic of Vietnam between 1965 and 1973 or if wounded, captured or killed in action during the above period.
Devices: 1960
Notes: Bar inscribed "1960-" is the only authorized version.

six-pointed star with cut lined, broad gold star points between and a central green disk with a map of Vietnam in silver surmounted with three painted flames in red, signifying the three regions of Vietnam. The reverse contains the inscription, *"VIET-NAM"* in a lined circle in the center with the name of the medal inscribed in Vietnamese text at the upper and lower edges separated by many short lines. The device, an integral part of the award, is a silver ribbon 28mm long on the suspension ribbon and 15mm long on the service bar inscribed, *"1960-   "* and was evidently intended to include a terminal date for the hostilities. Many examples of this medal are found with devices inscribed with other dates but the only version authorized for U.S. personnel is the one described.

⭐ Republic of Korea War Service Medal

The Republic of Korea War Service Medal was established in 1951 by the Government of the Republic of Korea for presentation to the foreign military personnel who served on or over the Korean Peninsula or in its territorial waters between June 27, 1950 and July 27, 1953. However, it was not approved for acceptance and wear by the U.S. until 1999. To be eligible for this award, U.S. military personnel must have been on permanent assignment or on temporary duty for 30 consecutive days or 60 non-consecutive days. The duty must have been performed within the territorial limits of Korea, in the waters immediately adjacent thereto or in aerial flight over Korea participating in actual combat operations or in support of combat operations. The 48 year interval between establishment and its formal acceptance represents the second longest period of time in

Republic of Korea War Service Medal
Service: All Services Instituted: 1953
Criteria: Service on the Korean Peninsula between 1950 and 1953
Devices: None
Notes: Above date denotes when award was authorized for wear by U.S. military personnel.
Notes: Not accepted by the United States Government for wear on the military uniform until 1999. *Some original 1953 medals had a taeguk in the center of the drape like the ribbon bar.

U.S. history between a significant national and military conflict and the award of an appropriate medal.

The medal is a bronze disk containing a map of the Korean Peninsula at top center over a grid of the world and olive branches on either side of the design. Below the map are two crossed bullets. In the center of the ribbon and earlier medal drapes *(1950's)*, is an ancient oriental symbol called a taeguk *(the top half is red and the bottom half is blue)*. The reverse contains the inscription, *"FOR SERVICE IN KOREA"* in English embossed on two lines with two small blank plaques on which the recipient's name may be engraved.

Medals of America Press **43**

★ Commemorative Medals - 235 Years of American Tradition

General Macomb Commemorative Medal

The United States Government, State Governments, Veterans Organizations, private mints and individuals have a long tradition of striking commemorative medals to recognize and honor specific military victories, historical events and military service to our great Republic. Until the 20th Century the United States did not issue military service medals recognizing service by veterans in the different wars, battles, campaigns or other significant military events.

The tradition of honoring U.S. military heroes began when the Continental Congress awarded Gold and Silver Medals to our triumphant commanders of The Revolutionary War. While these were struck as table display medals, General Gates the victor of Saratoga, wasted no time hanging his from a neck ribbon and wearing it for his official portrait. General Washington was awarded the first commemorative medal for driving the British from Boston and the first commemorative to a naval hero was awarded to Captain John Paul Jones. These Congressionally authorized medals were the forerunners of modern combat decorations. Some medals commemorate events such as the Mexican War and the Civil War, with reverse designs depicting famous battle scenes.

During the Mexican War certain states such as South Carolina issued medals to veterans of the state regiment which fought in the war. Other times, veterans formed societies and issued medals commemorating their service. Some of the more famous examples are the Grand Army of the Republic Reunion Medals and the Aztec Club Medal struck by veterans of the Mexican War. In some cases commanders during the Civil War issued privately commissioned commemorative medals such as the Kearney Cross.

Grand Army of the Republic Reunion Medal

The U.S. Mint regularly produces commemorative medals typically to celebrate and honor American people, places, events, including medals honoring military heroes, veterans and the Armed Services. For example, the Vietnam Veterans National Medal commemorates the courage and dedication of the men and women who served in that conflict.

The Missing in Action medal is a 15/16 inch miniature replica of the 3-inch medal authorized for presentation to the next-of-kin of American military and civilian personnel missing or other unaccounted for in Southeast Asia. The 200th anniversaries of the U.S. Army, Navy, Marine Corps and Coast Guard were also celebrated with the striking of national medals and the Persian Gulf National Medal honored Persian Gulf War veterans. Only bronze medals are available for sale to the public. For a complete listing of medals available from the U.S. Mint, call 1-800-872-6468.

Vietnam Commemorative Medal

While the federal government issues commemorative medals from the U.S. Mint, state and county governments who were particularly active after World War I used private mints and contractors to issue hundreds of different commemorative medals honoring World War veterans and providing a visible symbol of gratitude to their returning veterans. All of these medals were especially meaningful to both returning veterans and their families. Veteran's associations such as the American Legion, Veterans of Foreign Wars and even the Daughters of the Confederacy issued commemorative medals. For the past two hundred years these groups coupled with private mints have issued medals honoring historical military events, victories, deeds and service that honor American veterans.

Commemorative medals reflect typical American ingenuity and spirit, where local government, veterans associations and private leadership step forward to facilitate honoring service and deeds the federal government fails to recognize. In recent years the 75th Anniversary of World War I and the 50th Anniversary celebrations of both World War II and the Korea War were the occasions for well-deserved commemorative medals to honor the veterans of these conflicts. The most recent example is the Cold War Victory Commemorative Medal struck to fill the void created when Congress authorized a Cold War Victory Recognition certificate but never funded a medal.

Although unofficial in nature and usually struck by private mints or associations, commemorative medals provide a very tangible memento to honor all veterans and families for their service and sacrifice. On the next page are examples of commemorative medals from the last sixty years.

Cold War Victory Commemorative Medal

⭐ American Commemorative Medals for the Vietnam War

After the fall of the Republic and years passed, commemorative medals for veterans begin to appear in honor of significant events during the fighting. Not surprisingly, the first was a commemorative medal in honor of the Vietnamese Cross of Gallantry Unit Citation that came out along with one for the Civil Action Unit award.

A very unique commemorative medal honors those who fought during Tet and saw their victory turned to a defeat by the media. The U.S. made Commeoratives shown all are manufactured to same quality and specifications as official American military medals.

RVN Gallantry Cross Unit Citation Commemorative Medal

Qualifying Dates: 1965-1975

Criteria: Struck to honor all soldiers, sailors, marines, airmen and Allies who were awarded the RVN Gallantry Cross Unit Citation.

RVN Civil Action Unit Citation Commemorative Medal

Qualifying Dates: 1965-1975

Criteria: Struck to honor all soldiers, sailors, marines, airmen and Allies who were awarded the RVN Civil Action Honor Unit Citation.

Combat Action Commemorative Medal

Qualifying Dates: 1941-TBD

Criteria: Struck to honor all soldiers who served in Combat.

Vietnam Service Commemorative Medal

Qualifying Dates: 1960-1975

Criteria: Struck to honor all soldiers who served in South Vietnam or in direct support.

Presidential Unit Citation Commemorative Medal

Qualifying Dates: 1941-TBD

Criteria: Struck to honor all members of the U.S. Armed Forces who recieved the Presidential Unit Citation.

Meritorious Unit Citation Commemorative Medal

Qualifying Dates: 1941-TBD

Criteria: Struck to honor all members of the U.S. Armed Forces who recieved the Meritorious Unit Citation.

TeT Offensive Commemorative Medal

Qualifying Dates: 1968

Criteria: Struck to honor all, U.S. and Allied Forces who served during the 1968 TeT Offensive.

Airborne & Air Assault Commemorative Medal

Qualifying Dates: 1960-1975

Criteria: Struck to honor all Soldiers who made airborne or air assault operations.

Medals of America Press

★ Issue of U.S. Medals to Veterans, Retirees and their Families

How to Request the DD214

Veterans of any United States military service may request medals never issued (the majority of WW II veterans for example) or replacement of medals which have been lost, stolen, destroyed or rendered unfit through no fault of their own. Requests may also be filed for awards that were earned but, for any reason, were never issued to the veteran. A good example is the Korea Defense Service Medal which was recently approved and back dated to cover everyone who served in Korea after 1954. More than 2 million former service personnel are now authorized this medal. The next-of-kin of deceased veterans may also make the same request for the medals of their veteran family member.

The National Personnel Records Center, Military Personnel Records *(NPRC-MPR)* is the repository of millions of military personnel, health, and medical records of discharged and deceased veterans of all services during the 20th century. Information from the records is made available upon written request *(with signature and date)* to the extent allowed by law. Please note that NPRC holds historical Military Personnel Records of nearly 100 million veterans. The vast majority of these records are paper-based and not available on-line.

There are two ways for those seeking information regarding military personnel records stored at NPRC (MPR). If you are a veteran or next-of-kin of a deceased veteran, you may now use vetrecs.archives.gov to order a copy of your military records. For all others, your request is best made using a Standard Form 180. It includes complete instructions for preparing and submitting requests.

Using the vetrecs.archives.gov Requests for the issuance or replacement of military service medals, decorations, and awards should be directed to the specific branch of the military in which the veteran served. However, for Air Force *(including Army Air Corps)* and Army personnel, the National Personnel Records Center will verify the awards to which a veteran is entitled and forward the request with the verification to the appropriate service department for issuance of the medals.

The Standard Form (SF 180), Request Pertaining to Military Records, is recommended for requesting medals and awards. Provide as much information as possible and send the form to the NPRC address shown on this page.

1. How to Obtain Standard Form 180 *(SF-180)*, Request Pertaining to Military Records

    A. Download and print a copy of the SF-180 in PDF format by going to: http://www.archives.gov/facilities/mo/st_louis/military_personnel_records standard_form_180.html#sf.

    B. Write to **The National Personnel Records Center** 9700 Page Avenue, St. Louis, Missouri 63132.

    The SF 180 may be photocopied as needed. You must submit a separate SF 180 for each individual whose records are being requested.

2. Write a Letter to Request Records

    If you are not able to obtain SF-180, you may still submit a request for military records by letter. The letter should indicate if the request is for a specific medal(s), or for all medals earned. It is also helpful to include copies of any military service documents that indicate eligibility for medals, such as military orders or the veteran's report of separation *(DD Form 214 or its earlier equivalent)*. Federal law [5 USC 552a(b)] requires that all requests for information from official military personnel files be submitted in writing. Each request must be signed *(in cursive)* by the veteran or his next-of-kin indicating the relationship to the deceased and dated *(within the last year)*. For this reason, no requests are accepted over the internet.

    Requests must contain enough information to identify the record among the more than 70 million on file at NPRC (MPR). Certain basic information is needed to locate military service records. This information includes:

- The veteran's complete name used while in service, Service number or social security number
- Branch of service

    If the request pertains to a record that may have been involved in the 1973 fire, also include:
- Place of discharge
- Last unit of assignment
- Place of entry into the service, if known

Key addresses for information are:

National Personnel Records Center
1 Archives Drive
St. Louis, MO 63138

In case of a problem or an appeal write to:

U.S. Army Human Resources Cmd
Awards Division
Attn: AHRC-PDP-A
1600 Spearhead Ave.
Fort Knox, KY 40122-5408

★ Vietnam Campaign Medals & DD214 Examples

Good Conduct Medals	National Defense Service Medal
U.S. Vietnam Service Medal	Vietnam Campaign Medal
RVN Gallantry Cross Unit Citation	

```
4. MAILING ADDRESS (Include ZIP Code)
OSHKOSH   GARDEN    NEBRASKA    69154
5. ORIGINAL DD FORM 214 IS CORRECTED AS INDICATED BELOW:
ITEM NO.                           CORRECTED TO READ
         SEPARATION DATE ON DD FORM 214 BEING CORRECTED: 1969/11/07
  24     DELETE:  VIETNAM SERVICE MEDAL//
         ADD:  PURPLE HEART//COMBAT INFANTRYMAN BADGE//ARMY GOOD CONDUCT MEDAL//REPUBLIC
         OF VIETNAM MEDAL W/DEVICE (1960)//REPUBLIC OF VIETNAM GALLANTRY CROSS W/PALM UNIT
         CITATION//REPUBLIC OF VIETNAM CIVIL ACTIONS HONOR MEDAL FIRST CLASS UNIT
         CITATION//EXPERT MARKSMANSHIP QUALIFICATION BADGE W/RIFLE BAR
         (M-14)//SHARPSHOOTER MARKSMANSHIP QUALIFICATION BADGE W/MACHINE GUN BAR
         (M-60)//MARKSMAN MARKSMANSHIP QUALIFICATION BADGE W/RIFLE BAR (M-16)//VIETNAM
         SERVICE MEDAL W/TWO BRONZE SERVICE STARS//NOTHING FOLLOWS
```

Occasionally, a DD214 discharge needs to be corrected and this soldier's DD214 is a good example showing the Vietnam Service Medal was deleted and replaced with an entry at the end of the update form showing it was to have 2 campaign stars. This corrected form does an excellent job spelling out his awards and badges.

```
ITEM NO                            CORRECTED TO READ
         SEPARATION DATE ON DD FORM 214 BEING CORRECTED:  27 OCT 70
  24     DELETE: VSM//BSM//ARCOM
         ADD:  VIETNAM SERVICE MEDAL W/3 BRONZE SERVICE STARS//REPUBLIC OF VIETNAM
         GALLANTRY CROSS W/PALM UNIT CITATION BADGE//PURPLE HEART//ARMY COMMENDATION
         MEDAL W/"V" DEVICE//BRONZE STAR MEDAL W/"V" DEVICE AND FIRST OAK LEAF
         CLUSTER//NOTHING FOLLOWS
```

This DD214 discharge corrections deletes the abbreviations; VSM//BSM//ARCOM and spells out full name with the appropriate devices. In this case there is a big difference between a BSM and ARCOM with no devices and the corrected verisons that show the awards were for valor as opposed for meritorious service and that there were 2 awards of the Bronze Star Medal *(Oak Leaf Cluster)*

```
24 DECORATIONS MEDALS BADGES COMMENDATIONS CITATIONS AND CAMPAIGN RIBBONS AWARDED OR AUTHORIZED
NDSM              VCM      VSM     ARCOM    CIB    AIR MEDAL    2 O/S BARS
                  BSM      SPS (M-14)
```

This soldier's Vietnam era discharge is typical of abbreviations: NDSM is National Defense Service Medal; the VCM is the RVN Vietnam Campaign Medal; the VSM is the Vietnam Service Medal but missing the campaign stars and it is difficult to tell how many campaign stars he rates on his service medal without knowing when he was there. If you know the dates of his service in Vietnam you can compute the campaign stars from the table listed on the page describing the Vietnam Service Medal. ARCOM is the Army Commendation Medal, CIB, the Combat Infantryman Badge and Air Medal (AM) is correct. The 2 overseas service bars tell you he spent a year in Vietnam so he will have at least 2, up to 4 campaign stars depending on the period. The BSM is the Bronze Star Medal and SPS is for a Sharp Shooters Badge. The Vietnamese Cross of Gallantry Unit Citation is missing.

Basic Vietnam Military Awards

Arrival in Vietnam -
When a soldier first arrived in Vietnam and joined his unit he was authorized his Branch insignia, Unit Patch, National Defense Service Medal and Marksmanship badge.

After 30 days in Vietnam -
This Infantry soldier is awarded the Vietnam Service Medal after 30 days in country and may have qualified for the Combat Infantryman's Badge.

After Six months in Vietnam -
This Infantry soldier is authorized the South Vietnam Campaign Medal after six months in country and may have qualified for other awards.

After One Year in Vietnam -
This Infantry soldier may also be authorized the Good Conduct Medal at the end of his year of service in Vietnam if approved by his Commander.

Medals, Badges and Insignia U.S. Army Vietnam

U.S. Army Vietnam Display Cases

Vietnam Insignia

Medals

Sharpshooter w/Bar

Brass Plates

Patches

Campaign Battle Stars

Commemorative Medals

Army Branch Insignia

Display Cases

Vietnam 1965-1975
Over 3,403,000 Americans served in Vietnam during the 10 years of fighting. Their devotion to duty and combat record was extraordinary. Only after the US military withdrew after signing a peace accord did South Vietnam fall to the Communist who ignored the peace accord.

Vietnam -
This II Field Force soldier pictured on the radio personalized his award display case with medallions, his unit patch, his ribbons, skill badges and rank. He added two commemorative medals to represent that he had been in combat action and one to represent his RVN Gallantry Cross Unit Citation.

Vietnam -
This Patriotic Combat Medic Specialist 5 served 18 months and 5 campaigns in Vietnam plus reserve service.

Vietnam -
This Infantry CPL's handsome oak display case shows distinguished service in the First Infantry Division, the "Big Red One."

Vietnam -
This Artillery Recon Sgt. served in MACV and ARVN units and was decorated by both. Commemorative medals for Unit awards balance a terrific personal display.

Vietnam -
This Patriotic Transportation Specialist served 18 months and 5 campaigns in Vietnam plus reserve service.

Medals of America Press 49

U.S. Army Vietnam Award Displays

Letters

I joined the 5th Infantry "Red Diamond" Division in 67 and was alerted for Vietnam deployment March 1968. We reorganized as 1st Brigade Separate with Colonel Glikes as CO. After intensive training we loaded vehicles on railroad cars and arrived at Quang Tri, in July. August we moved into "Leatherneck Square" bordered by Con Thien, Cam Lo, Dong Ha, Gio Linh. My unit, D Co., 1-11 Inf was patrolling north of Con Thien when we ran into dug-in NVA units and got pinned down. C Company and tanks from 1-77 came charging in and we ran the NVA out of their holes. We conducted battalion-size operations all over the demilitarized zone until November when we moved to AO Marshall Mountain near Quang Tri City doing routine patrols with the 1st ARVN Division. It was a year I will never forget nor the guys I served with!

Vietnam -
This Military Intelligence Specialist 5th Class severed in Korea, Europe and Vietnam and rounds out his decorations and service medals with a 1968 Tet Offensive commemorative medal and RVN Gallantry Cross Unit Award.

Vietnam -
This First Sgt. severed in the First Air Cavalry Division and the 11th Armored Cavalry Regt. in Vietnam. He has Army Aircrew wings and has been awarded the Distinguished Flying Cross.

Vietnam -
This former Infantry Battalion Commander displays his miniature medals with Airborne wings and CIB. A neat arrangment since the miniatures can be removed and worn on formal occasions.

Vietnam -
This Warrant Officer displays his wings, hat badge, rank, badges and ribbons from his uniform.

Vietnam -
This Gunner Sgt. proudly displays his unit creast of the 14th Artillery along with his ribbons and medals.

Vietnam -
A platoon Sgt. from the 196th Infantry Brigade of the Americal Division displays his unit crest, CIB and medals over his unit awards and rank Insignia.

Vietnam -
This Transportation Corps Specialist 5th Class has his Aircraft Crew Member wings, earned as a door gunner, over his decorations and service medals.

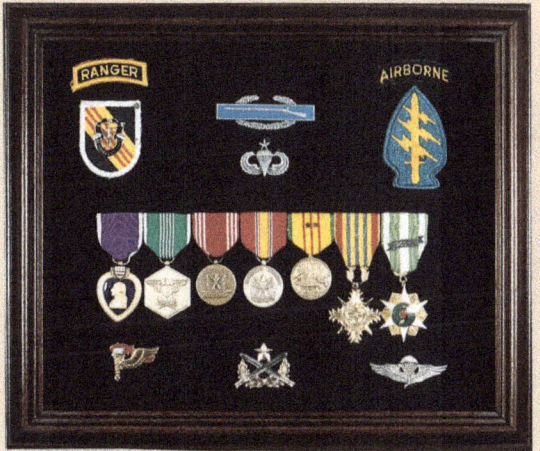

Vietnam -
This 5th Special Forces soldier displays his CIB, Senior Parachute Badge and Ranger Tab over his Medals and South Vietnamese Ranger and Special Forces Parachute Badge.

Vietnam -
This First Air Cavalry Division veteran's family mounted his multiply awards of the Purple Heart Medal ahead of his Bronze Star as personal choice in his memorial flag case.

Medals of America Press

Bibliography

Adjutant General of the Army- American Decorations 1862-1926, 1927
Belden, B.L. - United States War Medals, 1916
Borthwick, D. and Britton, J. - Medals, Military and Civilian of the United States, 1984
Boatner III, Major Mark M. - Military Customs and Traditions
Borts, L.H. - United Nations Medals and Missions, 1997
Crocker, US Army *(Ret)*, LTC Lawrence P. - Army Officer's Guide 42nd Edition
Crocker, US Army *(Ret)*, LTC Lawrence P. - Army Officer's Guide 45th Edition
Dept. of Defense Manual DOD 1348.33M - Manual of Military Decorations & Awards, 1996
Campbell, J. Duncan - Aviation Badges and Insignia of the United States Army, 1913-1946, 1977.

Dorling, H.T. - Ribbons and Medals, 1983
Emmerson, William H. - Encyclopedia of the United States Army Insignia and Uniform
Fisher, Jr., Ernest F. - Guardians of the Republic
Fisch, Jr., Arnold and Wright, Jr., Robert K. - The Story of the Noncommissioned Officer corps, The Backbone of the Army
Foster, Frank - Complete Guide to United States Army Medals, Badges and Insignia, 2004.
Foster, Frank - Military Medals of America, 2019.
Foster, Frank - United States Army Medals, Badges and Insignia, 2011.
Foster, Frank and Borts, Lawrence - Military Medals of the United States, 7th Edition 2010.

Foster, Frank and Sylvester, John - The Decorations and Medals of the Republic of Vietnam and Her Allies, 1950-1975, 1995.
Gleim, A.F.- United States Medals of Honor 1862-1989, 1989
Inter-American Defense Board - Norms for Protocol, Symbols, Insignia and Gifts, 1984
Jacobsen, Jr. Jacques Noel - Regulations and Notes for the Uniform of the Army of the Unites States, 1917
Katcher, Philip - The American Soldier - US Armies in Uniform, 1775 to Present
Kerrigan, E. - American Badges and Insignia, 1967
Kerrigan, E. - American Medals and Decorations, 1990
Kerrigan, E. - American War Medals and Decorations, 1971
Kredel, Fritz and Todd, Fredrick P. - Soldiers of the American Army, 1775-1954
Maguire, Jon A. - Silver Wings, Pinks and Greens, 1994
Military Service Publishing Co. - The Officer's Guide 1948, April Edition
Morgan, J. L. Pete -United States. Military Patch Guide, 2006
National Geographic Magazine, December, 1919
National Geographic Society - Insignia and Decorations of the U.S. Armed Forces, 1944
Oliver, Ray - "What's In A Name?," 1983.
Rosignoli, Guido - Badges and Insignia of World War II, 1980
Rosignoli, G. - The Illustrated Encyclopedia of Military Insignia of the 20th Century
Rush, USA (Ret), CSM Robert S. - NCO Guide
Simon and Schuster - Official Guide to the Army Air Forces, 1944
Smith, Richard W. - Shoulder Sleeve Insignia of the U.S. Armed Forces, 1981.
Strandberg, J.E. and Bender, R.J. - The Call to Duty, 1994
Smith, Richard W. Shoulder - Sleeve Insignia of the U.S. Armed Forces, 1981
Spink, Barry L. - "A Chronology of the Enlisted Rank Chevron of the United States Air Force," 1992
Thompson, James G. - Decorations, Medals, Ribbons, Badges and Insignia of the United States Marine Corps, 1998
Troiani, Don, Coates, Earl J., and Kochan, James L. - Don Troiani's Soldiers in America
U.S. Army Regulation 670-1 - Wear and Appearance of Army Uniforms and Insignia, May, 2000
U.S. Army Regulation 600-8-22 - Military Awards, 1995
U.S. Army Regulation 600-35, 1944.
U.S. Army Regulation 672-5 - Military Awards, 1990.
Vietnam Council on Foreign Relations - Awards & Decorations of Vietnam, 1972

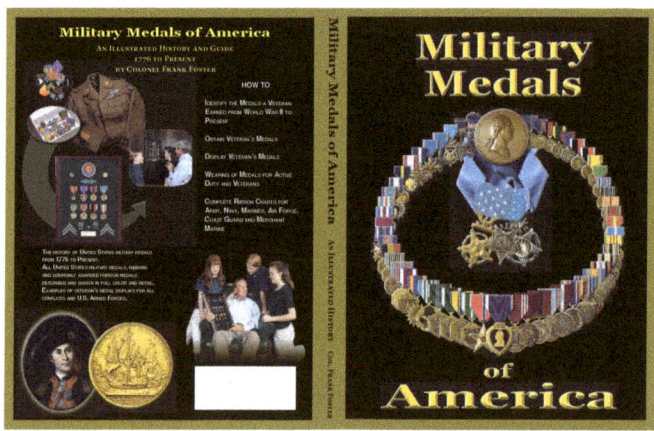

Abbreviations for Awards

AM	Air Medal	JSAM	Joint Service Achievement Medal
ACM	American Campaign Medal	JSCM	Joint Service Commendation Med
ADSM	American Defense Service Medal	KSM	Korean Service Medal
ASM	Antarctic Service Medal	KCM	Kosovo Campaign Medal
AFEM	Armed Forces Expeditionary Medal	KLM(K)	Kuwait Liberation Medal (Kuwait)
AFRM	Armed Forces Reserve Medal	KLM(SA)	Kuwait Liberation Medal (Saudi Arabia)
AFSM	Armed Forces Service Medal	LM or LOM	Legion of Merit
AAM	Army Achievement Medal	M or M Dev	Letter "M" Device
ARCOM	Army Commendation Medal	V or V Dev	Letter "V" Device
GCM or AGCM	Army Good Conduct Medal	MHA	Medal for Humane Action
AOM	Army of Occupation Medal	MH or MOH	Medal of Honor
ARCAM	Army Reserve Components Ach. Medal	MSM	Meritorious Service Medal
ARCOTR	Army Reserve Components Overseas Tng	MUC	Meritorious Unit Commenadation
ASR	Army Service Ribbon	NDSM	National Defense Service Medal
ASUA	Army Superior Unit Award	NPDR	NCO Professional Development Rib
APCM	Asiatic-Pacific Campaign Medal	NOL	Netherlands Orange Lanyard
BF	Belgian Fourragere	OLC	Oak Leaf Cluster
BA, AH or BAH	Bronze Arrowhead	OSR	Overseas Service Ribbon
OLC or BOLC	Bronze Oak Leaf Cluster	PDR	Philippine Defense Ribbon
BSS or BCS	Bronze Service Star	PIR	Philippine Independence Ribbon
BSM	Bronze Star Medal	PLR	Philippine Liberation Ribbon
CIB	Combat Infantryman Badge	POW	POW Medal
CMB or MB	Combat Medical Badge	PU	Presidential Unit Citation
DDSM	Defense Distinguished Service Medal	PH	Purple Heart
DMSM	Defense Meritorious Service Medal	VCM	Republic of Vietnam Campaign Ribbon
DSSM	Defense Superior Service Medal	SS	Silver Star
DFC	Distinguished Flying Cross	SM	Soldier's Medal
DSC	Distinguished Service Cross	SWASM	Southwest Asia Service Medal
DSM	Distinguished Service Medal	UNSM	United Nations Service Medal
EAMECM or EAME or ETO	European-African-Middle Eastern Campaign Medal	VUA	Valorous Unit Award
EFMB	Expert Field Medical Badge	VSM	Vietnam Service Medal
EIB	Expert Infantryman Badge	WACSM	Women's Army Corps Service Medalw
FF	French Fourragere	WWIVM	World War I Victory Medal
HSM	Humanitarian Service Medal	WWIIVM	World War II Victory Medal
JMUA	Joint Meritorious Unit Award		

MEDALS of AMERICA Press
Est. 1976

Other Great Medals and Insignia Books All Available at WWW.MOAPress.com or on Amazon

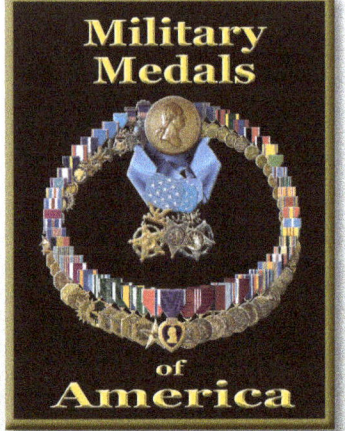
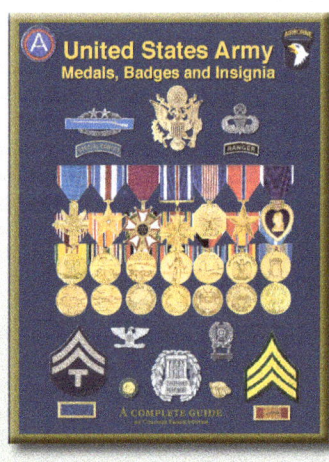

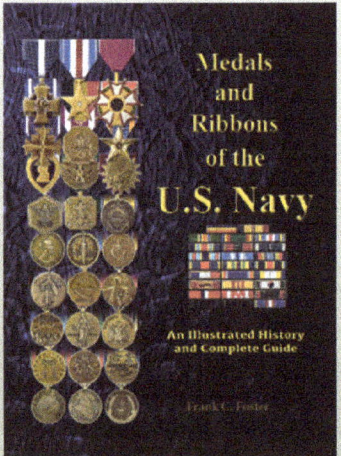

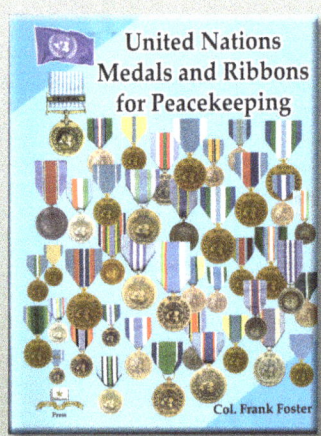
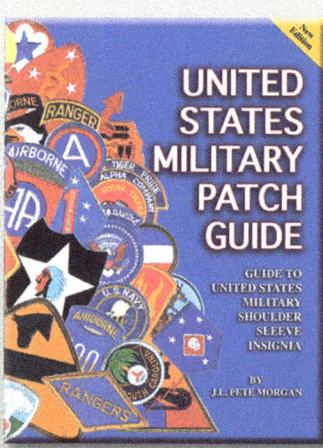

America's Best Medal and Ribbon Wear Guides All Available at WWW.MOAPress.com or on Amazon

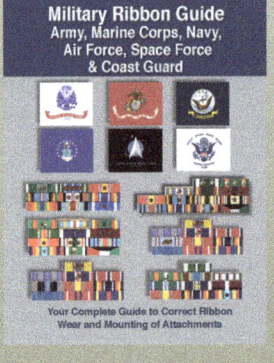

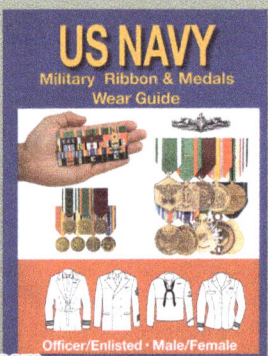
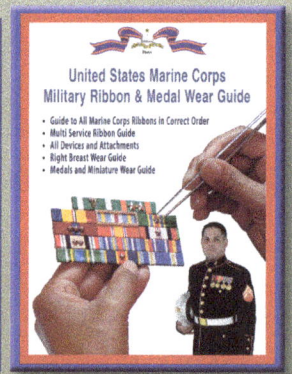

www.ingramcontent.com/pod-product-compliance
Lightning Source LLC
Chambersburg PA
CBHW051320110526
44590CB00031B/4415